Activities for Preschool and Kindergarten Children

I'm Ready To Learn

by Mary E. Wolfgang

& Corinne Mullen

A PARENT/CAREGIVER BOOK

INSTRUCTO/McGraw-Hill

Malvern, Pennsylvania 19355

Credits:
Cover and page illustrations by Patricia Traub
Page design by Kim Morrow

Library of Congress Cataloging in Publication Data

Wolfgang, Mary E.
   I'm ready to learn.

   "A Parent/caregiver book."
   Bibliography: p. 144
      1. Education, Preschool.   2. Kindergarten.
3. Learning.   4. Creative activities and seat work.
I. Mullen, Corinne.   II.Title.
LB1140.3.W64   1982   372'.21   82-17201
ISBN 0-07-530373-6

Printed in the United States of America

10 9   8   7   6   5   4   3   2

contents

contents

contents

contents

introduction

Watching a young child blossom and helping that flowering occur can be among life's most rewarding experiences for any parent or teacher. Persons who live and work with young children usually want to help them to achieve the fullest possible development. Parents are especially concerned these busy days with providing "quality" time for themselves and their children. The question arises, though, what kinds of activities would be the most valuable in this quality time?

We would suggest that even the most humdrum, everyday chores and activities can provide quality moments filled with learning experiences for the young child. How does one turn chores, such as sorting the laundry, putting away groceries, or cleaning out a cupboard, into meaningful learning activities for children? What are some ways to help children fully develop their abilities, especially when they may have some learning problems? What are some handy games and easy activities for leisure moments that can help a child to master new skills? Are there any skills (beyond the ABC's) which help a child to do better with beginning schooling that a parent can help to build at home during the early years?

The following pages provide some interesting answers to the above questions not only for parents but also for teachers, aides, and volunteers in the school setting.

This book of activities is designed to provide a solid foundation of home and school experiences to prepare the 3- to 6-year-old child for success in beginning school skills. However, this information may not be fully utilized, or organized, without the help of an adult.

Consider the example of three-year-old Johnny, walking down the street with his father who is taking a letter to the mailbox. On his own, Johnny may notice, feel, and/or experience many things, such as the warm sunshine, birds, nuts, pine cones, sewer covers, ant hills, and puddles. But it is only with interpretation and elaboration by his father that Johnny can understand what he is experiencing more fully. Johnny's father may point out different kinds of birds or nuts to Johnny, stimulating him to think more about the world around him and to better organize it in his mind. What made the puddle? Why is the sewer cover there? How are the birds alike or different? Why are there no nuts in the area without trees? How many ants do you think live there?

Parents, and later teachers, through the quality and content of their intentions and activities usually plant the seeds, cultivate the growth, and enjoy the fruition of their children's readiness for learning.

I'm Ready to Learn presents many everyday activities which are directly related to skills needed to do well in school. The elementary subjects of reading, writing, and arithmetic have been examined, and preparatory skills which help children develop readiness for school have been analyzed. These readiness skills can be fostered by use of the activities presented in the following pages.

Activities will be presented to develop the following skills: *remembering what you see* (visual memory), *seeing differences in shapes* (visual discrimination), *remembering order and placement of shapes* (visual discrimination of spatial orientation), *large and small muscle control* (perceptual motor abilities), *seeing and describing large and small details* (visual observation and interpretation), *labeling* (vocabulary building), *understanding prepositions, hearing differences in sounds* (auditory discrimination), and *repeating a story and following verbal directions* (auditory retention). These are skills required for school success. They are the "readiness for learning" skills.

Wide Range of Individual Differences

In any given group or class of young children, there is a wide variety of differences in the experiences and abilities of those children. Some children arrive at the school door having already developed many readiness for learning skills and are prepared to "go to the head of the class." Other children need help to develop some or many of these skills before, during, and after their early school experiences.

These readiness for learning activities can be adapted and used in many ways. They can be used at home by parents who are interested in early education and school success. They can be used with whole classes of preschool children or with small groups. Or these activities can be used with the individual child who is experiencing a particular learning problem.

Remembering What You See

Remembering what has been seen, or visual memory, requires the child to keep in his or her mind's eye a mental picture for a period of time. The first signs of this skill can be seen in the young infant (about six to twelve months of age) who can find a favorite toy which he or she has seen hidden under a blanket. The baby holds a primitive mental image of the toy in its mind long enough to retrieve it. This remembering skill becomes more complex as the child grows, and games such as "peek-a-boo" and "hide-and-seek" are ways in which the infant strengthens his or her memory skills.

Some preschool children have difficulty with remembering what they have seen because they get easily distracted, or they get lost in fantasy, or they are not able to remember more than one item at a time. Remembering things that have been seen is particularly important for the school-age child in developing basic skills. The child must be able to retain a mental image of the

9

introduction

ABC's before he or she can begin to remember the specific sounds associated with each letter or remember patterns of letters which form words.

Remembering Order and Placement of Shapes

The ability to see likenesses and differences between objects and groups of objects is one which is often taken for granted by adults, but it is a major developmental task for younger children. The child's development of intelligence is based on his or her ability or organize information about the world in which he or she lives. The child first begins to understand such fundamental group differences as family members and nonfamily members, and later, living and nonliving things, and boys and girls. In the preschool years, children usually learn to group objects by the fundamental characteristics of size, shape, and color.

The ability to organize objects and experiences into groups is based on the ability to see similarities and differences in objects. In early primary math, the concept of sets is based on the child's ability to group similar objects together. In beginning reading, the child must often group together words with the same beginning sounds. Many everyday experiences at home and at school can help prepare the child for a better understanding of likenesses and differences.

Seeing the Same Shape When It Has Been Moved

The child's ability to place objects in order helps him or her to better understand the organization of the world around him or her. Some precocious preschool children, having many opportunities to handle a wide variety of objects and toys, begin to put them in order by size or by a particular quality such as shape or texture. More often, however, children learn this ability by watching another child or an adult put objects in order. The most common beginning ways of ordering objects is to order them by size and shape.

The young child learns to order objects by manipulating them and by watching how others handle and order the objects. Much practice with hands-on objects is needed before children can hold in their mind's eye a mental picture of common ways of ordering objects. This skill is a requirement for holding in one's mind the correct order of letters, words, and also numbers. For a child to remember the correct order of the letters in his or her name, that child needs to have had many previous experiences with putting things in order. An important part of remembering the correct order of things requires that the child gain the ability to remember a mental picture of a whole object, a scene, or a set of objects and be able to tell when something has been changed.

To correctly copy shapes, numbers, letters, and words (common tasks for preschool and primary grade children), not only correct order but also correct placement of shapes must be remembered. A very common learning problem which occurs in the early school grades is the reversal of letters, or mirror writing. E is written like Ǝ , and R like Я . Practice with correct placement of real, touchable objects can help children prepare for the later, more abstract pencil and paper tasks of formal schooling.

Reproducing Simple Designs and Patterns

The young infant usually discovers his or her hands at about four to eight months. Discovery of the hands moves from a random process of movement to eventual realization that one can cause things to happen by using one's hands and eyes together. (For example, the baby can cause the bell on its cradle gym to ring by first seeing it and then by directing the hand toward it.)

The ability to use eyes and hands together develops gradually over the preschool years. Parents and teachers can help this development by providing model patterns for the child to copy. Later the child will be able to keep a mental picture of a pattern in his or her mind and reproduce it. This skill is necessary for the child to put together the letters in his or her name and to begin reading words.

Large and Small Muscle Control

Children progress from the first awkward steps toward numerous developmental stages until, by school age, they can usually control their large body movements well and can engage in physical games with other children. Children learn all about the world and about themselves through large amounts of play using their bodies and senses, especially in the first seven years of life. Some children arrive at the classroom door with more advanced physical abilities than others. This may be the result of inherited abilities or of much physical play and practice or both. Physical abilities and good control help the child develop self-confidence and a good feeling about him- or herself in relation to peers.

Development and control of the hand muscles are particularly important for school success. Most school tasks call for successful use of paper and pencil. There are many everyday activities to help children develop and strengthen these muscles.

Seeing and Describing Large and Small Details

The newborn baby notices only very large movements, usually connected with bright lights and brightly colored objects. As the child grows, he or she

11

introduction

gradually learns to see and understand more and more. The ability of the young child to see, label, and mentally organize many objects and experiences in his or her environment will help develop the child's memory and verbal ability — two skills necessary for school success.

Labeling

Usually a baby's first recognizable words are "MaMa" or "DaDa" and usually are heard during the second half of the first year of life. In two more years, young children usually have acquired hundreds more words or labels. These words become organizers for the child's experiences and help to promote his or her intellectual growth. Ability to label objects in spoken words is a prelude to the ability to label objects in beginning reading.

Grouping and Describing

After simple labeling, comes labeling of objects or events which share some relationship with each other, such as objects centered around eating (spoon, fork, plate, glass) or bath time (soap, tub, sponge). These label groups serve to further organize the child's learning.

Although children can sometimes group objects together out of their own initiative and attempts to make sense out of their world, they can often benefit from the help of adults. Parents and teachers can model the appropriate grouping of objects and children then can follow their examples.

Understanding Prepositions

Prepositions, such as *inside, in front of, over, beside,* and *between,* indicate abstract relationships between items which are often unrelated. Usually it takes a great deal of practice with the use of prepositions before children can understand and use them properly. Prepositions are very important to the child in the school setting. The child must be able to understand the meaning of spoken prepositions before he or she can understand written prepositions. Prepositions are also very important for following directions, both verbal and written.

Use of prepositions, such as *in/out, over/under,* and *up/down,* help the child to understand the meaning of his or her body in relation to space and of objects in relation to space. Piaget describes this task of understanding spatial relations as a major thrust of the preschool years — first through motor play and later through the use of words.*

*Weiker, David P; Rogers, Linda; Adcock, Carolyn; and McClelland, Donna; *The Cognitive Oriented Curriculum.* ERIC — NAEYC. Urbana, IL; 1977.

Remembering What You Hear

The first consistent sounds that impress the young infant are often the singing of lullabies by its mother. Some children develop listening as their primary mode of learning about the world. Others learn about the world more through the sense of sight. Some children are turned off to listening and learning through active responses by the overuse of television, by an understimulating environment, or by a genetic or physical difficulty in listening.

Skills in listening and remembering what is heard are important to function well in school. Practice in remembering what they hear is very helpful to most young children. The activities developed for this section center on everyday experiences and use common objects to help you and your child focus on and further develop these important listening skills.

Hearing Differences in Sounds

The ability to hear differences in sounds is more a discrimination skill than a remembering skill. For many children, the ability to detect likenesses and differences in sounds is much more difficult than detecting likenesses and differences in things that they can see. Much of the teaching in schools depends on the children's ability to listen and detect differences in sounds.

Repeating a Story and Recalling Verbal Directions

The language which a child hears and makes his or her own serves as an organizer for developing knowledge about the surrounding world. As the child's intelligence develops, so does his or her ability to remember and repeat more complex stories and directions.

It is just as important for the adult to invest time and energy listening to the child as it is for the child to learn to listen to the adult. This not only enables the parent or teacher to understand the child better, but it also allows the adult to clarify misunderstandings expressed in the child's language. The parent or teacher who consciously listens to a young child's stories models the value of learning through listening.

Activities for Children with Learning Disabilities and Special Needs

Learning disabilities have become more widely recognized in the last decade than ever before. Consequently, parents, teachers, and physicians are beginning to identify particular learning problems at younger and younger ages.

13

introduction

Often parents feel at a loss wondering not only why their child has a learning disability, but also, once it is diagnosed, what they can do to help their child. This book provides activities which parents can easily do to help their child begin to master some of the most common learning disabilities through daily interactions with the child.

The most common learning disabilities, and the most common problems that generally interfere with beginning school success, cluster around the following areas: visual perception, visual motor learning and auditory learning. These areas are further described in Appendix A, page 140.

The greatest benefit of these everyday activities for the learning disabled child is the individual encouragement and support the child can receive in overcoming his or her problem in learning from a concerned parent or teacher. The major help to parents provided by these activities is a handy, easy reference for using everyday materials in activities which will help them to help their child. These pages address the question of "What can I do to help my child?"

Using these activities in the school setting relates to Public Law 94-142 which addresses mainstreaming and requires the least restrictive learning environments for children with special individual needs. Thus, teachers are now working with a wider variety of children, and many children ages three to seven can benefit from individual use of the activities developed in this book. Also, many learning disabled children have difficulties in developing particular visual and auditory abilities, and these areas are the ones which can be developed through the activities in this book. Parents of children with special needs can easily become involved in supporting school goals by doing these activities to promote "readiness for learning" skills.

Observing Learning Chart

The Observing Learning Chart (Appendix B, page 143) is designed for keeping a progress record of children in a preschool or early childhood class. Information concerning the abilities or needs of the individual students can easily be recorded by an aide or volunteer. With this profile, the teacher can then choose related activities to help build and develop particular skill areas.

A sample Observing Learning Chart is on the next page. For each activity used, one sheet would be prepared. All the children's names would be listed and information on strengths and problems would be noted for each child.

OBSERVING LEARNING

ACTIVITY _Tray Play_

Child's Name	Date	Check for Success	Strengths or Special Comments	Problems or Difficulties
alan	9/21	✓	good memory	
Becky	9/21		tried hard, remembered	easily distracted, got frustrated
Cindy	9/22	✓	remembered details	
David	9/22	✓	excellent!	
Ellen	9/23		socessful with 5, then 6 objects	needs very quiet area
Frank	9/24		too much fantasy	could not keep mind on objects
Kevin	9/25	✓	good job	needed a lot of encouragement

Each activity in this book is coded to answer the functional questions which you must ask before you sit down and begin any learning activity with your child.

The codes will provide you with the answers to the questions:
"Where can we do this activity?"
At home and in the classroom.
At the grocery store. In the car.

and "How much time will the activity take?"

To answer these questions, the following symbols are used:

Time
◐ 10 minutes or less
◑ 10-30 minutes
● 30 minutes or more

Where
☐ Home or School
🚗 Car
☐ Grocery Store
⩗ Playground
🐻 Zoo
○ Anywhere

15

chapter 1
remembering what you see
(visual memory)

clotheshorse

GOAL   To help your child remember what he or she sees.

MATERIALS _____

None.

PROCEDURE _____

1. Tell your child to close his or her eyes and to name two things he or she is wearing.

2. Repeat this activity with your child asking for three, then four, items until he or she can name four or five articles of clothing.

TIME _____

Five minutes or less.

EVALUATION _____

This activity is a success when your child can close his or her eyes and tell you four things he or she is wearing.

RELATED ACTIVITIES _____

Other family members could easily join in. Children frequently love it when you close your eyes and try to tell them what they are wearing.

OBSERVING LEARNING _____

My child's favorite part of this activity was _____

_____

_____

Comments _____

_____

_____

groceries galore

GOAL

To help your child grow in the ability to remember what he or she has seen.

MATERIALS

A few groceries (not more than five) from your next trip to the store.

PROCEDURE

1. Ask your child to help you put the groceries away. Use the ones you've selected.

2. After the five groceries have been put away by your child, ask him or her to tell you what the groceries were.

TIME

About five to ten minutes.

EVALUATION

This activity is a success when your child can tell you what the five groceries were.

RELATED ACTIVITY

Use this activity when it's time to put toys away.

OBSERVING LEARNING

I think this activity helped my child because _____
_____
_____

My child's favorite part of this activity was _____
_____
_____

colors ▫ ◑

GOAL To strengthen your child's ability to remember what he or she sees.

MATERIALS

Scissors and red, blue, yellow, and green colored paper — can be wrapping paper scraps, construction paper, tissue paper.

PROCEDURE

1. Cut out four squares each of red, blue, yellow, and green paper.
2. You keep two squares of each color and give the other two to your child.
3. Now place three of your squares in a row to make a train.
4. Let your child look at your train.
5. Now cover it with a piece of paper.
6. Ask your child to make a train that looks like yours.

TIME

About thirty minutes.

EVALUATION

This activity is a success when your child can make a train like yours.

RELATED ACTIVITY

This could be done with blocks or toys instead of colored paper.

OBSERVING LEARNING

The part of this activity my child enjoyed most was _____

_____

_____

This activity helped my child because _____

_____

_____

□ ◔

can of fun

GOAL

To help your child grow in the ability to remember what he or she has seen.

MATERIALS

Can of shaving cream, index cards with a simple form on each one, such as a circle, square, triangle, rectangle, capital letter.

PROCEDURE

1. Place a "squirt" of shaving cream on the table in front of your child.
2. Hold up one of the index cards for your child to look at. Tell your child to look at it carefully.
3. Remove the picture and ask your child to make the picture of what he or she saw by moving his or her finger through the cream.

TIME

About five to ten minutes.

EVALUATION

This activity is a success when your child can reproduce the design seen on the card.

RELATED ACTIVITY

Try this activity using finger paint.

OBSERVING LEARNING

I think this activity helped my child because _____
_____
_____

The hardest part of this activity for my child was _____
_____

grocery tape

□ ◔

GOAL To help your child remember what he or she sees.

MATERIALS

Computerized tape from grocery store checkout, pen or pencil.

PROCEDURE

1. Circle one letter on the grocery tape.

2. Give the pen or pencil to your child and ask him or her to find and circle all the other letters that look just like the one you circled.

TIME

Five minutes or less.

EVALUATION

This activity is a success when your child can find all the letters on the grocery tape that match the one you circled.

Note: If your tape is very long, cut it into shorter sections and give your child one section.

OBSERVING LEARNING

I think this activity helped my child because _____

_____

_____

Comments _____

_____

_____

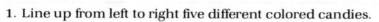

colored candies

GOAL

To help your child remember what he or she sees after being interrupted or distracted.

MATERIALS

Package of candies in various colors.

PROCEDURE

1. Line up from left to right five different colored candies.

2. Ask your child to look at each one as you point to it. You can say the name of each color.

3. Cover the candies and tell or sing a short, simple poem or song (such as "Twinkle, Twinkle Little Star") to your child.

4. Give your child five candies of the same colors you used.

5. Now ask your child to arrange his or her candies to look just like the ones you both looked at a minute ago.

6. Repeat this activity over several days.

TIME

Fifteen to twenty minutes.

EVALUATION

This activity is a success when your child can reproduce the color design.

RELATED ACTIVITY

Reverse roles and let your child be the "teacher".

OBSERVING LEARNING

I think this activity helped my child because _____

_____

_____

lots of money

GOAL

To help your child remember what he or she sees, and to lengthen his or her attention span.

MATERIALS

Two pennies, two nickels, two dimes, two quarters.

PROCEDURE

1. Line up from left to right one of each coin.

2. Direct your child to look at each coin as you point to it. You can name the coins.

3. Cover the coins and read a simple, poem to your child to interrupt the concentration.

4. Now, give your child five of the same coins, and ask your child to arrange his or her coins to look just like the ones you both looked at a minute ago.

5. Remove the cover from your coins. Have your child check his or her coin arrangement against yours. Is it correct?

6. Allow your child to correct his or hers to match yours.

TIME

Ten to fifteen minutes.

EVALUATION

This activity is a success when your child can remember the order of the coins.

OBSERVING LEARNING

A part of this activity that my child had difficulty with was _____

_____

_____

Comments _____

_____

_____

face fun

GOAL

To help your child remember what he or she sees.

MATERIALS

Eight index cards and a colored marker.

PROCEDURE

1. Draw a simple face on an index card, such as

2. Ask your child to turn his or her back while you draw four faces on another index card, one that matches Face 1 — the other three different, such as

3. Ask your child to find the face he or she looked at a minute ago — the matching face.

TIME

About fifteen to twenty minutes.

EVALUATION

This activity is a success when your child can select the "match" out of four possibilities.

RELATED ACTIVITY

This activity could be extended to stick figure bodies. Your child may want to try drawing, asking you to pick the matching face.

OBSERVING LEARNING

The hardest part of this activity for my child was _____

_____

_____

collage _____ □ ◐

GOAL   To help your child remember what he or she sees.

MATERIALS _____

Picture with many objects in it.

PROCEDURE _____

1. Show the picture to your child and talk about what is in picture.

2. Take away the picture.

3. Ask your child to name as many details in the picture that he or she can remember.

TIME _____

Fifteen to thirty minutes.

EVALUATION _____

This activity is a success when your child can name at least ten of the discussed items.

RELATED ACTIVITY _____

Read a story to your child, such as *Goldilocks and the Three Bears.* Find a picture which has many of the objects (the pieces of furniture, beds, chairs, bowls, etc.) mentioned in the story. Ask your child to find the objects.

OBSERVING LEARNING _____

The hardest part of this activity for my child was _____

_____

_____

From this activity, my child learned _____

_____

_____

□ ◑ —————————————————————————— # tray play

To help your child remember what he or she sees. **GOAL**

——————————————————————————————— **MATERIALS**

Tray with ten assorted objects — such as items found in the kitchen junk drawer.

——————————————————————————————— **PROCEDURE**

1. Have your child look at the tray carefully for five minutes.

2. Take the tray away.

3. Ask your child to name as many of the objects as he or she can remember seeing on the tray.

——————————————————————————————— **TIME**

Twenty minutes.

——————————————————————————————— **EVALUATION**

This activity is a success when your child can name nine or ten objects.

——————————————————————————————— **RELATED ACTIVITY**

A picture containing many objects could be shown instead of a tray of objects.

——————————————————————————————— **OBSERVING LEARNING**

This activity was a success for my child because _____

_____

_____

The hardest part of this activity for my child was _____

_____

_____

hidden animals ☐ ◑

GOAL To help your child remember what he or she sees.

MATERIALS _____

Storybook about animals, a piece of cardboard larger than the book with a one-inch hole cut out of the middle.

PROCEDURE _____

1. Read the story to your child, pointing out all the kinds of animals.

2. Have your child tell you the name of each animal he or she can remember.

3. As your child names the animal, show him or her that animal through the hole in the cardboard.

TIME _____

Fifteen to thirty minutes.

EVALUATION _____

The activity is a success when your child can randomly remember 8 out of 10 of the animals in the story.

RELATED ACTIVITIES _____

Use other books with easily identifiable objects. Also, your child might enjoy trying to remember the animals in the order they appeared in the story.

OBSERVING LEARNING _____

My child liked this activity because _____

_____

_____

The hardest part of this activity for my child was _____

_____

_____

chapter 2
remembering order and placement of shapes
(visual discrimination)

clothesline □ ◔

GOAL   To help your child see likenesses and differences.

MATERIALS

A clothesline or piece of string or yarn tied between two objects, such as chairs or tree branches. A box of items with many having one match (fabric scraps, wrapping paper scraps, magazine pages, or actual clothing). Clothespins or paper clips.

PROCEDURE

1. Place an item, such as a shirt, on the line and say to your child, "Can you find a shirt to hang up next to my shirt?"

2. Continue in this manner until you have the "clothesline" filled.

TIME

About five to ten minutes.

EVALUATION

This activity is a success when your child can match your objects on the line.

OBSERVING LEARNING

The hardest part of this activity for me was _____
_____
_____

I think this activity was good for my child because _____
_____
_____

☐ ◑ _____ likenesses & differences

GOALS

To help your child see likenesses and differences, and to see the relationship of parts to the whole.

MATERIAL

Your child's favorite cereal box, when it's empty.

PROCEDURE

1. Cut a rectangle from the empty box — be sure it includes the picture part of the box. Then cut the rectangle into several puzzle pieces.

2. Ask your child to put the puzzle together.

TIME

Ten to twenty minutes.

EVALUATION

This activity is a success when your child can put the pieces together.

RELATED ACTIVITIES

Puzzles can be made from any of your child's favorite pictures or birthday or holiday cards.

OBSERVING LEARNING

How long did it take your child to do this activity? _____

_____

_____

Did you or your child have any problems with this activity? _____

_____

_____

letters in the news _____ □ ◑

GOAL To help your child grow in the ability to see likenesses and differences in capital and small letters.

MATERIALS _____

Front page of a newspaper or a page from a magazine, a crayon or pencil.

PROCEDURE _____

1. Tell your child that you are looking for three capital letters. Circle each one as you find it.

2. Now tell your child that you are looking for three small letters. Circle each one as you find it.

3. Now ask your child to be the detective and find three capital letters. Circle each one as it is found.

4. Now ask your child to do the same with three small letters.

TIME _____

Ten to fifteen minutes.

EVALUATION _____

This activity is a success when your child can recognize the differences between capital and small letters.

OBSERVING LEARNING _____

I think this activity helped my child because _____

_____

_____

Comments _____

_____

_____

□ ◔ ────────────── # wallpaper match

GOAL

To help your child grow in the ability to match things that are identical.

MATERIALS

Scraps of various wallpaper patterns (many stores will give away the outdated books), index cards, glue.

PROCEDURE

1. Cut and mount on index cards identical pieces of wallpaper. Make four matches.

2. Hold one card in front of your child and ask him or her to find the match.

3. Do the same with the other sets until the four matches have been made.

TIME

About five minutes.

EVALUATION

This activity is a success when your child can match like patterns.

RELATED ACTIVITIES

As your child grows in facility with this skill, the number of pairs may be increased. Wrapping paper from a birthday party is a good source of material.

OBSERVING LEARNING

I think this activity helped my child because _____

_____

_____

Comments _____

_____

_____

plenty of pennies
□ ◔

GOAL To help your child see likenesses and differences.

MATERIALS

Six pennies, six nickels, six dimes, six quarters.

PROCEDURE

1. Line up the six pennies from left to right so that the first penny is heads up, the next four are tails up, and the last one is heads up.

2. Point to the first penny on the left and say to your child, "See this penny. Find me another one over here that looks just like this one."

3. Do the same activity with the nickels, dimes, and quarters.

4. Reverse roles and let your child set up the coins.

TIME

About five minutes.

EVALUATION

This activity is a success when your child can match the two coins out of six.

RELATED ACTIVITY

Give your child six to ten coins and ask him or her to set them up in a row where they all match.

OBSERVING LEARNING

I think this activity did/did not help my child because _____

_____

_____

The hardest part of this activity for my child was _____

_____

_____

□ ◑ _____ # colored blocks

To help your child see differences in shapes of objects. **GOAL**

MATERIALS

Colored wooden blocks in various shapes, such as a triangle, square, rectangle, and circle.

PROCEDURE

1. Line up five blocks, two that are an identical match and three that are different. See example below.

2. Put your finger on the first block at the left and say to your child, "See this block. Now find me another one over here just like this one."

3. Do this several more times with other blocks.

TIME

Ten to fifteen minutes.

EVALUATION

This activity is a success when your child can find "another one just like this one."

RELATED ACTIVITY

Colors could be substituted as an alternative.

OBSERVING LEARNING

This activity helped my child because _____

_____

_____

The hardest part of this activity for my child was _____

_____

magnetic letters

GOAL
To help your child see the sameness in two letters out of three.

MATERIALS _____

A double set of magnetized letters and numbers.

PROCEDURE _____

1. Select five letters, two that are identical, three that are not. Place them on the refrigerator or any metal surface.

2. Put your finger on one of the two matching letters and ask your child to find the other one just like it.

3. Do this several times—then ask your child to point to a letter for you to find the matching letter.

TIME _____

Ten to fifteen minutes.

EVALUATION _____

This activity is a success when your child can find the match.

RELATED ACTIVITIES _____

Make up your child's name with the magnetic letters and have your child make his or her name just like the one you made. No magnetic letters? Cut apart letters from cardboard advertising.

OBSERVING LEARNING _____

The hardest part of this activity for my child was _____

_____

_____

Comments _____

_____

_____

plastic put-togethers

GOAL

To help your child see likenesses and differences.

MATERIALS

Plastic containers of various sizes and shapes.

PROCEDURE

1. Spread all your plastic containers on your kitchen table or floor.

2. Show your child a square container, and ask him or her to find all the others that are the same as this one.

3. Stack all the square containers together.

4. Repeat with round containers, different size containers, bowls and lids, matching all the ones that are the same and separating the ones that are different.

TIME

From ten to thirty minutes.

EVALUATION

This activity is a success when your child can separate containers that are the same from those that are different.

RELATED ACTIVITIES

This activity could also be done with pots and pans or unbreakable dishes.

OBSERVING LEARNING

My child's favorite part of this activity was _____

_____

_____

The hardest part of this activity for my child was _____

_____

_____

picking pasta

GOAL To help your child see likenesses and differences.

MATERIALS

Four small plastic margarine dishes, macaroni noodles, rigatoni, shells, rice, or dried beans.

PROCEDURE

1. Place a different dried food or pasta in each of three dishes.
2. In the fourth dish, place a food that is the same as one of the foods in one of the other three dishes.
3. Have your child find the two dishes that contain the same type food.
4. Rearrange the dishes and repeat.
5. Change the food so that a different kind is in two dishes and repeat steps 3 and 4.

TIME

About fifteen minutes.

EVALUATION

This activity is a success when your child can correctly match the two foods that are the same.

RELATED ACTIVITIES

The number of dishes could be increased to five or six. The types of food could be varied to include raisins or cereals.

OBSERVING LEARNING

This activity was good for my child because _____

_____

_____

While doing this activity, my child said (or did) the following: _____

_____

chapter

3 seeing the same shape when it has been moved

(visual discrimination of spatial orientation)

cars and trucks □ ◔

GOALS To help your child see the difference in similar objects and recall their order and placement.

MATERIALS

Five toy cars or trucks or toys or trucks cut from magazines.

PROCEDURE

1. Ask your child to make a "convoy" of cars or trucks, all pointing in the same direction.

2. Have your child turn his or her back while you turn around one of the cars or trucks.

3. See if your child can recognize the trick and make it right.

TIME

About five to ten minutes.

EVALUATION

This activity is a success when your child can arrange the convoy in the same direction.

RELATED ACTIVITIES

This activity could be tried with blocks or shoes.

OBSERVING LEARNING

I think this activity helped my child because _____

_____

_____

My child's favorite part of this activity was _____

_____

_____

round and round

GOAL

To help your child see differences in shapes or forms depending on where they are placed.

MATERIALS

About ten buttons or paper circles of various sizes.

PROCEDURE

1. Tell your child to look at all the buttons and select the smallest one.

2. Put the rest of the buttons in order from smallest to largest, moving from left to right.

3. Mix up the buttons.

4. Ask your child to pick out the largest button, and then arrange in largest to smallest order from left to right.

TIME

About five to ten minutes.

EVALUATION

This activity is a success when your child can arrange the buttons in a left to right sequence from smallest to largest and also largest to smallest.

RELATED ACTIVITIES

This activity could be tried with blocks or milk cartons of various sizes.

OBSERVING LEARNING

I think this activity helped my child because _____

_____

_____

Comments _____

_____

_____

Seeing The Same Shape
When It Has Been Moved   41

spoons

□ ◔

GOAL To help your child see things in smallest to largest order.

MATERIALS

A set of measuring spoons or a set of dry measuring cups.

PROCEDURE

1. Ask your child to arrange the spoons in order from the smallest to the largest.

2. Now ask your child to arrange the spoons in order from the largest to the smallest.

TIME

About five minutes.

EVALUATION

This activity is a success when your child can arrange the objects in order from smallest to largest and then from largest to smallest.

RELATED ACTIVITIES

This activity could also be tried using nails or screws.

OBSERVING LEARNING

The hardest part of this activity for my child was _____

_____

_____

Comments _____

_____

_____

silverware

GOAL

To help your child see the differences in forms depending on how they are placed.

MATERIALS

Five forks.

PROCEDURE

1. Line up the forks in a left to right pattern similar to the one diagrammed below.

2. Put your finger on the first one and ask your child to: "Find one over here just like this one."

3. Rearrange the forks and try the activity again.

TIME

About ten minutes.

EVALUATION

This activity is a success when your child can find the matching fork.

RELATED ACTIVITIES

This activity may also be tried with spoons or knives.

OBSERVING LEARNING

I think this activity helped my child because _____

_____

_____

Comments _____   _____

_____   _____

_____   _____

saw/was ☐ ◑

GOAL To help your child see the differences in similar words.

MATERIALS

Index cards and a colored marker.

PROCEDURE

1. Print the word "saw" on an index card. On four other index cards write the following words — one to a card: *was asw saw swa*.

2. Line the cards up from left to right — *saw* being the first word.

3. Pointing to the first *saw*, say to your child, "Look at this. Now find me another over here just like this one."

TIME

Ten to twenty minutes.

EVALUATION

This activity is a success when your child can pick out the match.

RELATED ACTIVITIES

Use other three-letter words, such as *sat, mat, pin,* and *pan.* As your child experiences success with three-letter words, move on to four- and five-letter words.

OBSERVING LEARNING

I think this activity helped my child because _____

_____

_____

Comments _____

_____

_____

□ ◑ _____ # wonderful water

GOAL

To help your child see the difference in volume.

MATERIALS

Three matching glasses, water, pitcher.

PROCEDURE

1. Fill two glasses with the same amount of water.

2. Fill the third glass with less water.

3. Ask your child to look at the three glasses and to find the one glass that needs more water.

4. Let your child fill this glass using a small pitcher until the water level is the same as in the other two.

TIME

Fifteen to thirty minutes.

EVALUATION

This activity is a success when your child can find and fill the third glass to match the other two.

RELATED ACTIVITY

This same activity could be tried with sand and plastic containers.

OBSERVING LEARNING

I think this activity helped my child because _____

_____

_____

A better way to do this activity would be to _____

_____

_____

catalog match

GOAL To help your child match one object to another.

MATERIALS

Two identical catalogs, cardboard, glue, and scissors.

PROCEDURE

1. Paste two identical catalog pages containing LARGE pictures on the cardboard.

2. Cut one page into four or five pieces.

3. Have your child match the cut pieces to the whole catalog page.

TIME

About ten minutes.

EVALUATION

This activity is a success when your child can correctly match the cut pieces of the catalog picture to the whole page, placing the pictures in the correct position.

RELATED ACTIVITIES

This activity can be done using more complex pictures and with more pieces as your child gains success with matching the simpler pictures.

OBSERVING LEARNING

I think this activity helped my child because _____
_____
_____

A difficulty my child had with this activity was _____
_____
_____

□ ◑ _____ # upside down family

To help your child see the shape of the person who is in the wrong position.

MATERIALS

Pictures of four to six family members cut out of a magazine and backed with cardboard.

PROCEDURE

1. Place all of the family members upside down, except one. Use the table or floor as your space.

2. Ask your child to find the one person who is not in the same position as everyone else, and fix it to be the same as the rest of the family.

3. Repeat with different positions: standing up, lying down, leaning sideways.

TIME

Ten to fifteen minutes.

EVALUATION

This activity is a success when your child can correctly identify the out-of-place person and fix it to look like the rest of the family.

RELATED ACTIVITY

This activity could also be done with animal pictures.

OBSERVING LEARNING

This activity helped my child because _____

_____

_____

A problem we had with this activity was _____

_____

_____

Seeing The Same Shape
When It Has Been Moved   47

simple simon blocks

GOALS   To help your child find a block that is out of place and then to correct it.

MATERIALS

A set of small blocks of different sizes and shapes.

PROCEDURE

1. Make a pattern with four blocks.

2. Make a copy of the pattern and point out to your child that the second set of blocks looks just like the first set.

3. Change one block's position as your child watches.

4. Tell him or her to fix it to look like the first pattern.

5. Have your child cover his or her eyes as you change another block's position. Ask him or her to find the one that's out of place and fix it.

6. Next change two blocks, and then three.

7. Have your child find and fix them.

TIME

Fifteen to twenty minutes.

EVALUATION

This activity is a success when your child is able to find the block that is out of place and to put it in the correct position.

RELATED ACTIVITY

The child can set the pattern and have the adult find the block that is "wrong".

OBSERVING LEARNING

My child liked this activity because ⎯⎯⎯⎯⎯⎯⎯⎯⎯⎯⎯⎯

⎯⎯⎯⎯⎯⎯⎯⎯⎯⎯⎯⎯⎯⎯⎯⎯⎯⎯⎯⎯⎯⎯⎯⎯⎯⎯⎯⎯

⎯⎯⎯⎯⎯⎯⎯⎯⎯⎯⎯⎯⎯⎯⎯⎯⎯⎯⎯⎯⎯⎯⎯⎯⎯⎯⎯⎯

chapter 4
reproducing simple designs and patterns
(visual motor integration)

making jewelry _____ □ ◑

GOAL   To help your child grow in the ability to coordinate hands with eyes.

MATERIALS _____

Macaroni with large holes or straws cut into small pieces, pieces of string or yarn long enough for bracelets or necklaces, tape, any colored paper.

PROCEDURE _____

1. Make a needle-like point on a piece of yarn by wrapping tape around one end. Knot the other end.

2. String the macaroni or straws onto the yarn, leaving enough string or yarn to tie ends together. (Some help is usually needed to tie the ends together.)

TIME _____

Thirty minutes.

EVALUATION _____

This activity is a success when your child can complete a "bracelet" or a "necklace".

RELATED ACTIVITY _____

You could cut shapes (such as triangles, rectangles, and circles) out of paper and string them with the macaroni.

OBSERVING LEARNING _____

This activity was worthwhile because _____

_____

_____

My child enjoyed this activity because _____

_____

_____

□ ◑ ──────────────────────────────── # toothpicks

GOAL

To help your child grow in the ability to coordinate hands and eyes.

──────────────────────────────── **MATERIALS**

Toothpicks.

──────────────────────────────── **PROCEDURE**

1. Arrange six toothpicks in a specific shape or design.
2. Ask your child to make the same design, using toothpicks.
3. Make another design and have your child reproduce it.

──────────────────────────────── **TIME**

Ten to fifteen minutes.

──────────────────────────────── **EVALUATION**

This activity is a success when your child can reproduce the same design you made.

──────────────────────────────── **RELATED ACTIVITIES**

Instead of toothpicks, use macaroni, rice, or beans.

──────────────────────────────── **OBSERVING LEARNING**

This activity was worthwhile for my child because _____

_____

_____

My child's favorite part of this activity was _____

_____

_____

blocks ☐ ◔

GOAL To help your child grow in the ability to coordinate hands with eyes.

MATERIALS

Paper blocks or squares cut out of any colored paper.

PROCEDURE

1. Arrange three paper blocks side by side in front of your child.

2. Now ask your child to arrange three more blocks just like yours.

3. After your child has mastered three blocks (or squares of colored paper), arrange four side by side in the same manner. Have your child copy your pattern.

TIME

Five to ten minutes.

EVALUATION

This activity is a success when your child can copy the design of four paper blocks or squares.

RELATED ACTIVITY

Have your child string beads following an example that you have made.

OBSERVING LEARNING

My child enjoyed this activity because _____

_____

_____

From doing this activity, my child learned _____

_____

_____

□ ◑ _____ # sandpaper fun

To help your child grow in the ability to coordinate hands and eyes.

GOAL

MATERIALS

Sandpaper (medium grade), crayons.

PROCEDURE

1. On a piece of sandpaper, use a crayon to draw a simple design, such as an oval or square.

2. Let your child trace the shape using his or her finger.

3. Give your child a piece of sandpaper and a crayon and say, "Now make a picture just like mine."

4. Continue with more sandpaper and crayons using shapes such as triangles, rectangles and double figures, such as X U.

TIME

Fifteen to thirty minutes.

EVALUATION

This activity is a success when your child can reproduce on sandpaper the specific designs.

RELATED ACTIVITIES

This activity can be done outside on the sidewalk using chalk or a paint brush and water.

OBSERVING LEARNING

From doing this activity, my child learned _____

_____

Comments _____

_____

fun with clay

GOAL To help your child grow in the ability to coordinate hands with eyes.

MATERIALS _____

Clay.

PROCEDURE _____

1. Show your child how to work with the clay.
2. Make a simple snake out of a piece of clay.
3. Ask your child to make one just like yours.
4. Continue, but make other shapes such as a ball or a basket.

TIME _____

Thirty minutes.

EVALUATION _____

This activity is a success when your child can reproduce your clay snake.

RELATED ACTIVITY _____

Let your child use an old rolling pin and cookie cutters with clay.

OBSERVING LEARNING _____

I think this activity helped my child because _____

_____

_____

My child's favorite part of this activity was _____

_____

_____

□ ◑ _____ # cereal designs

GOAL

To help your child grow in the ability to coordinate hands and eyes.

MATERIALS

Box of dry cereal.

PROCEDURE

1. Using the cereal, make a simple design such as a rectangle.

2. Give your child some cereal and say, "Now make a design just like mine with your cereal pieces."

3. Continue making more designs — a circle, square, spiral, and so on.

TIME

Ten to twenty minutes.

EVALUATION

This activity is a success when your child can reproduce the rectangle.

RELATED ACTIVITIES

Have your child make up the designs and you copy them. Use pennies or buttons instead of cereal.

OBSERVING LEARNING

The hardest part of this activity for my child was _____

_____

_____

My child's favorite part of this activity was _____

_____

_____

first names first □ ◔

GOAL	To help your child grow in the ability to reproduce a simple design.

MATERIALS

Paper and pencil.

PROCEDURE

1. Print the letters of your child's first name — one at a time.

2. Have your child copy each letter after you.

3. If your child's name contains many letters or if your child has patience for printing only two or three letters, work gradually — every other day.

4. Continue this activity until your child can copy his or her entire first name.

TIME

About ten minutes.

EVALUATION

This activity is a success when your child can copy his or her first name.

RELATED ACTIVITIES

Use fingerpaints or watercolors and a paint brush and paper.

OBSERVING LEARNING

The hardest part of this activity for my child was _____

_____

_____

Comments _____

_____

_____

□ ◑ ————————————————— # doggie walk

To help your child develop coordination of hands with eyes. **GOAL**

————————————————— **MATERIALS**

Crayons and paper.

————————————————— **PROCEDURE**

1. Draw a stick dog figure at the left of the paper and a ball at the right of the paper.

2. Draw two parallel lines, about an inch apart, from the dog to the ball.

3. Tell your child that he or she is to take the dog to the ball with his or her crayon. Demonstrate by drawing your finger between the two lines.

4. Let your child use a crayon to draw a line between the dog and the ball.

————————————————— **TIME**

Ten to twenty minutes.

————————————————— **EVALUATION**

This activity is a success when your child can control the crayon and "stay on the road" between the two lines.

————————————————— **RELATED ACTIVITIES**

This activity can be made harder by curving the "road" or by making a simple maze. You can also include stick people and other animals going to houses, stores, parks, schools, and so on.

————————————————— **OBSERVING LEARNING**

This activity helped my child because _____

_____

_____

large and small muscle control

walk the plank

□ ◑ _____

To help your child grow in the use of large muscles.   **GOAL**

_____ **MATERIAL**

One four- to six-foot piece of board (wide enough to accommodate your child's feet when placed side by side).

_____ **PROCEDURE**

1. Place the board on a flat, even surface.

2. Work with your child on the following exercises:
   a. Walk all the way along the board.
   b. Walk backwards along the board.
   c. Turn around in the middle of the board and walk back to the end.

3. Encourage your child to practice each of these three skills, one at a time.

4. Take turns every now and then with your child.

_____ **TIME**

Fifteen minutes, but it will vary depending on the motor development of your child.

_____ **EVALUATION**

This activity is a success when your child can walk forwards and backwards on the board.

_____ **RELATED ACTIVITIES**

Let your child ask other family members and friends to try it with him or her.

_____ **OBSERVING LEARNING**

My child enjoyed this activity because _____

_____

_____

This activity helped my child because _____

_____

_____

yummy painting

GOAL To help strengthen finger and hand muscles.

MATERIALS

Large batch of instant pudding in your child's favorite flavor, large sheets of coated or glossy shelf paper, lots of newspapers.

PROCEDURE

1. Make the pudding with your child describing what you're doing.
2. Spread the newspapers on the table to collect spills.
3. Place the shelf paper over the newspapers.
4. Let your child go to town and paint on the shelf paper using the pudding.

TIME

Fifteen to twenty minutes.

EVALUATION

This activity is a success when your child uses his or her fingers and hands to make the designs, and can keep the pudding on the paper.

RELATED ACTIVITY

Use "real" fingerpaint. In a container, mix one tablespoon of powder tempera paint (for color), one-quarter cup of liquid starch, and one-quarter cup of mild liquid dish detergent.

OBSERVING LEARNING

The hardest thing about this activity for my child was

_____

_____

_____

uniquely yours

GOAL

To develop and coordinate hand muscles.

MATERIALS

Blunt scissors, 8- or 10-inch squares of white paper.

PROCEDURE

1. With your child, fold a square of paper into a triangle and then again into a smaller triangle.

2. Now cut along the edges and the fold line.

3. Open it up and see a lovely snowflake.

4. After making several with you, encourage your child to make some alone.

TIME

Five to fifteen minutes.

EVALUATION

This activity is a success when your child can fold the paper and manipulate the scissors to make a snowflake.

RELATED ACTIVITIES

Tape snowflakes to thread and string to hangers for a mobile. For variety, use square scraps of aluminum foil or foil wrapping paper.

OBSERVING LEARNING

This activity helped my child because _____

_____

_____

My child enjoyed this activity because _____

_____

_____

scissors strips ◻ ◑

GOAL   To give your child the opportunity to master the use of scissors and paste.

MATERIALS

Blunt scissors, paste, wrapping paper scraps, colorful magazine covers.

PROCEDURE

1. Show your child how to cut strips about one inch by eight inches from magazine covers or wrapping paper.

2. Show your child how to paste the ends of the strip together to form a circle.

3. Cut another strip and paste it around the circle to form the beginning of a chain. (Make sure you are explaining to your child what you're doing.)

4. Your child should do the cutting and pasting now to complete the chain.

5. Let your child decorate his or her room with the chain.

TIME

Fifteen minutes.

EVALUATION

This activity is a success when your child has completed a chain.

OBSERVING LEARNING

The best part of this activity for my child was _____

_____

My child had difficulty with _____

_____

_____

□ ◑ _____ **cut ups**

To help your child master or better control his or her small muscles. **GOAL**

_____ **MATERIALS**

Any scraps of paper, such as wrapping paper, newspaper or foil, blunt scissors.

_____ **PROCEDURE**

1. Fold a piece of paper in half.

2. Have your child fold another piece of paper in half

3. Have your child cut along the crease in and out. (Use your paper and another pair of scissors to demonstrate.)

4. Help your child open up the fold.

_____ **TIME**

Ten to fifteen minutes at a time.

_____ **EVALUATION**

This activity is a success when your child can manipulate and control the scissors.

_____ **RELATED ACTIVITY**

Do this activity on a snowy day and call the cut ups "snowflakes". String the snowflakes with thread and hang.

_____ **OBSERVING LEARNING**

The best part of this activity for my child was _____

_____

_____

We made this activity better by _____

_____

_____

left from right

GOALS To help your child distinguish and remember the difference between his or her left and right hands.

MATERIAL

A piece of yarn, ribbon, string, or lace.

PROCEDURE

1. Tie a "bracelet" ribbon on your child's right wrist.

2. Remind your child that the right wrist of his or her body has the bracelet.

3. Let your child see the difference by raising both hands. You say, "The one with the bracelet is your right hand and this is the 'left' over hand.".

4. Encourage your child to practice using his or her right and left hands.

5. Give directions to your child, such as "Lift your right arm." "Hand me the milk with your left hand."

TIME

Ten minutes initially. It may take several different blocks of time to help your child distinguish his or her left hand from the right.

EVALUATION

This activity is a success when your child knows the difference between his or her right and left hands.

RELATED ACTIVITY

Try to get this book from the library to read to your child, *Left, right, Left, right,* by Muriel Stanek.

OBSERVING LEARNING

The hardest part of this activity for my child was _____

_____

_____

colorful comics

GOAL

To help your child develop fine motor control of his or her hands and fingers.

MATERIALS

The comic page from a daily newspaper, crayons or colored pencils, 8½" x 11" paper, scissors, glue, and a large sheet of paper.

PROCEDURE

1. Ask your child to select his or her favorite comic strip.

2. Cut it out and glue it to a large sheet of paper.

3. Ask your child to color the strip, trying to stay within the lines.

TIME

Five to ten minutes.

EVALUATION

This activity is a success when your child can stay within the lines 80% of the time.

RELATED ACTIVITY

Any page in the newspaper can be "colored". Use the food pages, advertisements, or pictures from the entertainment section of children's movies.

OBSERVING LEARNING

The hardest part of this activity for my child was _____
_____
_____

My child enjoyed this activity because _____
_____
_____

down the path

GOAL To help your child control and direct a pencil or crayon.

MATERIALS

Crayon, pencil, and a section from the classified section of the newspaper.

PROCEDURE

1. Place the classified section horizontally on the table.

2. With a crayon, make a line right down the middle of the section, all the time talking to your child about trying to stay in the middle.

3. Ask your child to take his or her crayon and make a line down the middle of another classified section.

4. Now ask your child to draw a line down the middle of another classified section, using a *pencil.*

5. Do this two or three times with a pencil, using a different classified section each time.

6. Praise your child's efforts. It's hard for a five- or six-year-old to draw a line down the middle of something.

TIME

About fifteen minutes.

EVALUATION

This activity is a success when your child can draw a line down the middle of a classified section.

RELATED ACTIVITY

For variety, try this activity using printed paper or cardboard.

OBSERVING LEARNING

This activity helped my child by _____

_____

_____

□ ◑ ___ practice and patience

GOALS

To help your child learn to lace shoes and develop hand/eye coordination.

MATERIALS

A child's shoe with eyelets and a shoelace with good "tips" on it.

PROCEDURE

1. Place one shoe in front of your child as if he or she were going to put it on his or her foot.

2. Place yourself behind or beside your child and *slowly* show your child how you lace the shoe by going in and out of the eyelets.

3. Let your child have a try at lacing. Be patient and generous with your praise for your child's efforts. (This activity may take lots of practice and patience.)

TIME

Fifteen to thirty minutes.

EVALUATION

This activity is a success when your child can easily lace up the shoe.

RELATED ACTIVITY

When your child can lace the shoe, show him or her how to tie it, making sure you place the shoe as if the child were wearing it.

OBSERVING LEARNING

This activity helped my child because _____

_____

_____

My child enjoyed this activity because _____

_____

sand and salt

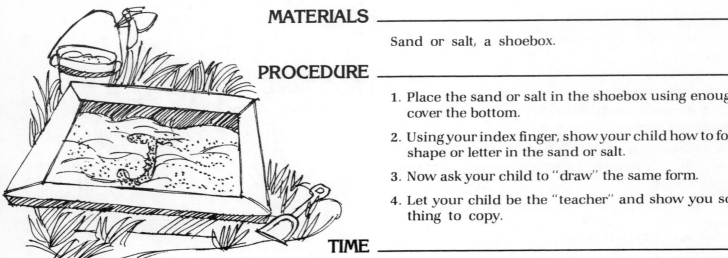

GOAL

To give your child practice in forming letters in a textural environment.

MATERIALS

Sand or salt, a shoebox.

PROCEDURE

1. Place the sand or salt in the shoebox using enough to cover the bottom.

2. Using your index finger, show your child how to form a shape or letter in the sand or salt.

3. Now ask your child to "draw" the same form.

4. Let your child be the "teacher" and show you something to copy.

TIME

Ten to fifteen minutes.

EVALUATION

This activity is a success when your child can reproduce a shape or letter in the sand or salt.

RELATED ACTIVITIES

Use wet sand in a plastic dishpan (the letters will last longer). Also try wet clay. Let dry and the letters will remain.

OBSERVING LEARNING

My child enjoyed this activity because _____

_____

_____

The hardest part of this activity for my child was _____

□ ◑ _____ # ball in a box

GOAL

To help your child grow in the ability to coordinate hands with eyes.

MATERIALS

Box about ten inches square, ball about three inches in diameter, tape or chalk.

PROCEDURE

1. Demonstrate throwing the ball into the box.

2. Let your child throw the ball into the box.

3. Now mark off certain distances (use tape or chalk). Begin two feet away from the box and increase the distance as your child can easily throw the ball into the box from each distance.

TIME

Five to fifteen minutes.

EVALUATION

This activity is a success when your child accomplishes getting the ball into the box.

RELATED ACTIVITY

Try throwing a bean bag into the box from certain distances.

OBSERVING LEARNING

My child had difficulty with this activity because _____
_____
_____

The best part of this activity for my child was _____
_____
_____

6

seeing and describing large and small details

(visual observation and interpretation)

□ ◔ ———————————————————————— # private eye

GOAL

To help your child grow in the ability to see large and small details.

MATERIALS

None.

PROCEDURE

1. Have your child accompany you to any room in your house.

2. Ask your child to look around the room and name every object he or she sees.

3. If your child needs help, point to objects missed and suggest that he or she first look at the floor and then up along one wall to the ceiling.

TIME

From five to ten minutes.

EVALUATION

This activity is a success when your child can name about five large objects (door, table) and five small objects (drawer handle, clock). Eventually ten to fifteen large and small objects can be named.

RELATED ACTIVITY

Try this activity while waiting for someone to come out of a store or while walking around the block or along a beach.

OBSERVING LEARNING

I think this activity helped my child because _____

_____

_____

Comments _____

sign reading

GOAL To help your child grow in the ability to see large and small details.

MATERIALS

Crayons, paper.

PROCEDURE

1. Prior to your next car ride together, draw two frequently seen traffic signs for your child (a stop sign and a railroad crossing sign).

2. Discuss each sign with your child.

3. When riding in the car, ask your child to tell you each time he or she sees one of the two signs you've talked about.

TIME

Fifteen minutes, plus the length of the car ride.

EVALUATION

This activity is a success when your child can recognize the two traffic signs you've chosen.

RELATED ACTIVITIES

Instead of traffic signs, look for certain stores (a gas station and a grocery store) when shopping or look for play equipment in parks or playgrounds.

OBSERVING LEARNING

My child's favorite part of this activity was _____

_____

_____

From doing this activity, my child learned _____

_____

_____

newspaper scavenger

GOAL

To help your child grow in the ability to see large and small details.

MATERIALS

Newspapers or magazines, paper, crayon, pencil or scissors.

PROCEDURE

1. Go through the magazine or newspaper and make a list of objects pictured.

2. Name for your child three or four items from your list.

3. Let your child go through the magazine or newspaper you have looked through and have him or her circle or cut out the three or four pictures named.

TIME

About fifteen minutes.

EVALUATION

This activity is a success when your child can find the three or four objects you named.

RELATED ACTIVITY

Instead of magazines or newspapers, try this activity during a long car ride. Name three or four objects for your child to look for during the ride.

OBSERVING LEARNING

My child enjoyed this activity because _____

_____

_____

The hardest part of this activity for my child was _____

_____

red car

GOAL To help your child grow in the ability to see large and small details.

MATERIALS

None.

PROCEDURE

1. Next time your child is traveling in the car with you, give him or her something specific to look for, such as red cars.

2. Vary the activity by looking for other colored cars, selecting colors with which your child is familiar.

TIME

Three to four minutes in the beginning, longer as child's interest grows.

EVALUATION

This activity is a success when your child can recognize a specific colored car.

OBSERVING LEARNING

My child's favorite part of this activity was _____

_____

_____

Comments _____

_____

_____

I see something

GOAL

To help your child grow in the ability to see large and small details.

MATERIALS

None.

PROCEDURE

1. Say, "I see something round and orange" (an orange in a bowl of fruit).

2. Have your child look around the room and guess what it is.

3. Take turns. Have your child be the one to say, "I see something _____," for you to guess what it is.

TIME

This may be played until your child becomes restless and loses interest.

EVALUATION

This activity is a success when your child can give you the answer to your description.

OBSERVING LEARNING

The hardest part of this activity for my child was _____

_____

_____

Comments _____

_____

_____

red, round, and little

GOAL
To help your child grow in the ability to see different colors, shapes, and sizes.

MATERIALS

Produce in a grocery store.

PROCEDURE

1. On a trip to the grocery store, have your child name or point out all the fruits that are red, green, or yellow.

2. Then ask him or her to point out fruits that are round or oblong, big or little.

3. Finally, using three criteria, ask your child to point out red (or green or yellow), round (or oblong), big (or little) fruits.

TIME

Five to fifteen minutes.

EVALUATION

This activity is a success when your child can name the fruits matching the characteristics of color, shape, and size.

RELATED ACTIVITIES

Extend this activity to include vegetables. When at home, name foods on the table that are of a certain color, shape, and size.

OBSERVING LEARNING

The hardest part of this activity for may child was _____

_____

_____

□ ◑

toys are special

GOALS

To help your child grow in the ability to see and to categorize large and small details.

MATERIALS

Playroom or area, variety of children's toys, containers for toys (cardboard boxes, toy boxes, shelves).

PROCEDURE

1. Select about ten toys of various colors and sizes.

2. Compare large and small toys (Examples: a toy box to blocks or large balls to small balls).

3. Place the large toys in one container (or area), small toys in another.

4. Categorize further by placing large toys with wheels in one container, small toys with wheels in another container.

TIME

Fifteen minutes.

EVALUATION

This activity is a success when your child can identify and categorize large and small toys.

RELATED ACTIVITIES

This makes a good activity when it is time to pick up toys. Also, select other characteristics (color, texture, shape) to sort by.

OBSERVING LEARNING

My child like this activity because _____

_____

_____

small, medium, and large _____ □ ◑

GOAL   To help your child understand the small-medium-large concept.

MATERIALS _____

Magazine pictures of babies, young children from ages three to ten, and adults (Mom and Dad).

PROCEDURE _____

Have your child place pictures of small people (babies) in one group, medium size people in another (young children) and large people (adults) in the third group.

TIME _____

Fifteen minutes.

EVALUATION _____

This activity is a success when your child can group items (small, medium and large) without great difficulty.

RELATED ACTIVITIES _____

Different sized dolls or trucks can be grouped according to small, medium and large sizes.

OBSERVING LEARNING _____

The part of this activity my child had difficulty with was _____

_____

_____

My child enjoyed this activity because _____

_____

_____

□ ◑ —————————————— # finger lickin food

GOAL

To help your child describe large and small details about food.

MATERIALS

Pictures from a magazine of a breakfast, lunch, or dinner, pieces of actual food.

PROCEDURE

1. Ask your child to name the different foods he or she sees in the picture.

2. Pick one of the foods and then ask your child to answer the following questions:
   What are words that tell how it looks?
   What are words that tell how it smells?
   What are words that tell how it tastes?
   What are words that tell how it feels?
   How does it sound when it is being cooked?
   How does it sound when it is being eaten?

3. Use pieces of actual food and ask the same questions.

TIME

Ten to fifteen minutes.

EVALUATION

This activity is a success when your child can use two or three words to describe sensory details about food.

RELATED ACTIVITIES

Describing the food can be done without pictures, using just real food. Or if the child knows the real food well, it can be done with the pictures alone.

OBSERVING LEARNING

This activity helped my child because ————————————————

————————————————

7

ability to label

(vocabulary building)

□ ◑ _____ # house hunt

GOAL

To help your child grow in the ability to identify objects in the home.

MATERIALS

None.

PROCEDURE

1. Say to your child, "Let's take a walk and see what we can find."
2. Explain to your child that you both are going to look for things made of a certain type of material; for example, things made of glass, or wood, or paper, or metal.
3. Tell your child what the material is.
4. When your child finds an object, let him or her touch it.
5. Ask your child to name each object he or she finds.

TIME

Five to fifteen minutes.

EVALUATION

This activity is a success when your child can name the objects found.

RELATED ACTIVITIES

On the house hunts, you could look for objects made with certain colors or textures.

OBSERVING LEARNING

This activity was worthwhile because _____

_____

_____

My child enjoyed this activity because _____

_____

seeing red

GOALS
To help your child grow in the ability to identify and label things.

MATERIALS
None.

PROCEDURE

1. Have your child accompany you to any room in your house.

2. Look around the room and say, "I see something red." Ask your child to guess what it is.

3. Continue in the same manner with the other colors: yellow, blue, green, orange, purple, brown, and black.

TIME
Fifteen to twenty minutes.

EVALUATION
This activity is a success when your child can locate and name the various objects described.

RELATED ACTIVITY
This activity could be tried with beginning consonants. For example, say to your child, "I see something that begins with the same sound that Mary begins with ... M-M-M."

OBSERVING LEARNING
The hardest part of this activity for my child was _____

_____

_____

This activity helped my child because _____

_____

□ ⏲ **labels**

GOAL

To help your child grow in the ability to name household objects.

MATERIALS

None.

PROCEDURE

1. While you are giving your child a bath, name the objects you use or ones you see in the bathroom: soap, water, faucet, toilet, sink, mirror, and individual toys.

2. When you are drying your child, see if he or she can point to and name the same objects named during the bath.

TIME

Five to ten minutes.

EVALUATION

This activity is a success when your child can name objects in the bathroom of your house.

RELATED ACTIVITY

Do this activity in any room of the house, using the objects in the room.

OBSERVING LEARNING

My child enjoyed this activity because _____

_____

_____

I think this activity helped my child because _____

_____

_____

going to the zoo

GOALS To help your child grow in the ability to identify and label animals found in the zoo.

MATERIALS

Paper, pencil or crayons, magazines or storybooks.

PROCEDURE

1. Take your child to the zoo.

2. Point out all the various kinds of animals.

3. When you are back home, ask your child to look through magazines or books and find pictures of the animals seen at the zoo.

TIME

About two hours.

EVALUATION

This activity is a success when your child can correctly identify pictures of animals in a magazine or book after a trip to the zoo.

RELATED ACTIVITY

On your trip to the zoo, suggest to your child that he or she draw a picture of one of the animals. Give him or her paper and pencils to do a drawing.

OBSERVING LEARNING

What did your child learn from this activity? _____

_____

_____

Comments _____

_____

_____

_____ on the playground

GOALS

To help your child grow in the ability to identify and label equipment on the playground.

MATERIALS

Playground equipment in a park.

PROCEDURE

1. Next time "there is nothing to do", take your child to a nearby park with a variety of playground equipment.

2. As your child moves from place to place, tell him or her the name of each piece of equipment (rainbow, gym, merry-go-round, slide, seesaw, etc.).

3. Ask him or her to name the pieces as he or she plays on each one.

TIME

About one hour.

EVALUATION

This activity is a success when your child can name the various pieces of playground equipment.

OBSERVING LEARNING

What did your child learn from doing this activity? _____
_____
_____

Comments _____
_____
_____

try it, you'll like it ⬛ ◕

GOAL   To help your child grow in the ability to label new foods.

MATERIALS _____

A fruit or a vegetable your child has not tasted before.

PROCEDURE _____

1. Next time you take your child to the grocery store with you, ask him or her to select a fruit or a vegetable he or she has never tried before.

2. Tell your child the name of the new food.

3. When you get home, fix the food for your child to try.

4. Ask your child to tell you the name of this "new" food.

TIME _____

About one hour.

EVALUATION _____

This activity is a success when your child can tell you the name of the new food.

OBSERVING LEARNING _____

My child enjoyed this activity because _____

_____

_____

Comments _____

_____

_____

□ ◑ _____ # hide and seek

GOALS

To help your child grow in the ability to identify and label objects in the home.

MATERIALS

Various objects found in the home, such as kitchen utensils, shoe, pencil, soap, and so on.

PROCEDURE

1. Hide about ten objects in your home.
2. Ask your child to find them.
3. As each object is found, ask your child to pick it up and tell you its name.

TIME

Fifteen minutes.

EVALUATION

This activity is a success when your child can name the objects when they are found.

RELATED ACTIVITY

Have your child look for specific things that are not hidden but classified by color, material, or shape; for example: things that are red, made of wood, shaped like a circle, and so on.

OBSERVING LEARNING

This was a good activity for my child because _____

_____

_____

Comments _____

_____

_____

laundry time

☐ ◔

GOALS To help your child grow in the ability to identify and label objects in the home.

MATERIALS

Child's laundry.

PROCEDURE

1. The next time you plan to do the laundry, have your child with you as you sort the clothes.

2. When you come across a piece of clothing that is your child's, help him or her name the item.

3. Ask him or her to tell you what part or parts of the body each item covers.

TIME

About ten minutes.

EVALUATION

This activity is a success when your child can correctly label the clothing and can explain where it belongs on the body.

RELATED ACTIVITIES

This activity can be done with the laundry of other family members or items found in certain rooms of the house (sheets, pillow cases, towels, facecloths, and so on).

OBSERVING LEARNING

What did your child learn from doing this activity? _____

_____

My child's favorite part of this activity was _____

_____

department store ads

GOAL

To help your child grow in the ability to label everyday items sold in a department store.

MATERIAL

Department store advertisements.

PROCEDURE

1. Help your child identify each of the items in the advertisement.

2. Then, take your child to the store and find the advertised items.

3. When you return home, use the advertisement to review with your child what you saw.

TIME

About ten minutes with the advertisement, plus time to go to the store.

EVALUATION

This activity is a success when your child can name the articles in the advertisement without your help.

RELATED ACTIVITY

Before going shopping for groceries, check the food advertisements with your child. On the trip, find some of the advertised items.

OBSERVING LEARNING

My child enjoyed this activity because _____

_____

This activity helped my child because _____

_____

community helpers

GOAL To help your child learn the names of the community workers with whom you often come in contact.

MATERIALS

Camera and film.

PROCEDURE

1. With their permission, take pictures of the people you deal with everyday: mail carrier, bank teller, gas station attendant, store clerk, and so on. Include as part of the picture the equipment they use — mail truck, gas pumps, cash register, and so on.

2. Show the pictures to your child.

3. Help your child name the workers, their equipment, and their occupation.

TIME

Will vary.

EVALUATION

This activity is a success when your child can easily name the community workers, their equipment, and their occupation.

RELATED ACTIVITIES

Storybooks or coloring books with pictures of community helpers could be used instead of photographs.

OBSERVING LEARNING

This was a good activity for my child because _____

_____

A difficulty we had with this activity was _____

_____

_____

chapter 8
(categorization)

grouping and describing

sink or swim □ ◔

GOAL   To help your child classify various objects as to whether they float or not.

MATERIALS

Various objects, such as corks, spoons, rocks, and plastic toys.

PROCEDURE

1. Scrub any object that normally is not one your child plays with at bathtime.
2. Let your child select a few to play with in the tub.
3. Talk to him or her about the ones that float and the ones that do not.
4. Encourage your child to separate the objects according to what floats and what does not.

TIME

Five to ten minutes.

EVALUATION

This activity is a success when your child can tell you which objects float and which do not.

RELATED ACTIVITIES

This activity could be tried at the sink or with a basin or a large bowl filled with water. Swimming pool could also be used. Let your child play with a natural sponge. Give it to him or her when dry and place it in the water. Let it stay in the water for awhile and as it sinks, ask your child what is happening. Make sure he or she understands why.

OBSERVING LEARNING

My child enjoyed this activity because _____

_____

_____

This activity helped my child because _____

_____

□ ⏱ ─────────────────────────────── # scents/smells

To help your child distinguish various smells. **GOAL**

─────────────────────────────── **MATERIALS**

Small containers and "smell" item, such as garlic, onion, lemon peel, spices, and perfumes or after-shave lotions.

─────────────────────────────── **PROCEDURE**

1. Work with your child to collect a variety of objects or foods having distinct odors (scents). Place them in individual containers.

2. Talk about each item's scent with your child.

3. Have your child close his or her eyes and guess what scent goes with what item.

4. Change the selection of items from time to time.

─────────────────────────────── **TIME**

Five to ten minutes.

─────────────────────────────── **EVALUATION**

This activity is a success when your child can tell you the source of the various scents.

─────────────────────────────── **RELATED ACTIVITY**

You guess for your child what items belong to what scents.

─────────────────────────────── **OBSERVING LEARNING**

The hardest thing about this activity was _____

_____

_____

The easiest thing about this activity was _____

_____

_____

sharp shoppers

GOALS To help your child classify products and to recognize words and symbols.

MATERIALS

A simple shopping list or pictures for your child the next time you go to the grocery store.

PROCEDURE

1. Make a simple shopping list (use pictures for a young child) for your child listing about five similar items.
2. Be specific, naming or showing the brands you prefer.
3. Talk to your child about the items on the list.
4. At the store, have the child find the items on the list.

TIME

Fifteen minutes.

EVALUATION

This activity is a success when your child can find the items on the list.

RELATED ACTIVITY

Go "shopping" using the grocery ads from a newspaper or a magazine. See how many of the items your child can locate in the store. Mark each off as it is found.

OBSERVING LEARNING

The thing I liked best about this activity was _____

_____

The thing my child liked best about this activity was __

_____

_____

polishing the apple

GOAL

To help your child practice the skill of organization.

MATERIALS

Three or four varieties of apples.

PROCEDURE

1. Discuss with your child the name and color of each apple.

2. Now have a "tasting" party. Invite other family members to join in.

3. Talk about the taste of each apple — sweet or sour? Talk about the texture — juicy or dry? crunchy or soggy? Which one does each person like?

TIME

Ten to fifteen minutes.

EVALUATION

This activity is a success when your child can tell you one or two things about each apple tasted.

RELATED ACTIVITY

Draw and color each apple sampled. Under the drawing, write down one or two descriptive words that your child tells you about each apple.

OBSERVING LEARNING

The hardest part of this activity for my child was _____

_____

_____

I think this activity helped my child because _____

_____

_____

color cloths

GOALS　To help your child recognize various colors.

MATERIALS

Swatches of solid colored fabric in red, blue, yellow, orange, green, and purple.

PROCEDURE

1. Give your child the swatch of red fabric and ask him or her to find as many objects of the same color as he or she can in the house.

2. When your child is pretty good at spotting red, change the swatch to blue and ask him or her to do the same thing.

3. Then, change to yellow, followed by orange, green, and purple.

TIME

Ten to fifteen minutes per color, per day. (Do only one color per day.)

EVALUATION

This activity is a success when your child can identify each color and find other objects of that color.

OBSERVING LEARNING

My child enjoyed this activity because _____

_____

_____

The hardest part of this activity for my child was _____

_____

_____

□ ◑ _____ **crayons**

To help your child classify crayons according to color. **GOAL**

_____ **MATERIALS**

Box of twenty-four or forty-eight crayons or a box of extra
or broken crayons, book entitled *Hailstones and Hailbut
Bones* by Mary O'Neill.

_____ **PROCEDURE**

1. Read one color poem from the book to your child each
   day.

2. Ask your child to put all the crayons that match the
   color poem in a group.

3. Each day after reading one color poem, group the
   crayons according to the color of each poem.

_____ **TIME**

About fifteen minutes.

_____ **EVALUATION**

This activity is a success when your child can group the crayons by color.

_____ **RELATED ACTIVITIES**

This activity could be done with various wrapping paper scraps or fabric
swatches. Read the poem "Color" by Christina G. Rossetti, and use it in the
same way the book was used.

_____ **OBSERVING LEARNING**

This activity helped my child because _____

_____

_____

My child's favorite part of this activity was _____

_____

_____

tasting party ☐ ◑

GOAL To help your child select a food that is not sweet.

MATERIALS

Three sweet-tasting foods, such as a pear, a peach, and an apple; one nonsweet food, such as a dill pickle.

PROCEDURE

1. Discuss with your child the name and color of each food to be sampled.

2. Now have a "tasting" party. Ask your child to describe how each food tastes. Encourage your child to go beyond the word "good".

3. Ask your child to tell you which food had a very different taste. Why was it different?

TIME

Twenty to thirty minutes.

EVALUATION

This activity is a success when your child can tell you the one food out of four that has a nonsweet taste.

RELATED ACTIVITIES

Draw and color each food tasted. Under the drawing, print the word your child used to describe the food. Vary the activity by using three chocolate foods and one nonchocolate food instead of the fruits and pickles.

OBSERVING LEARNING

The hardest part of this activity for my child was _____
_____

_____

From doing this activity, my child learned _____
_____

_____

□ ◐ ———————————————— # grab bag

To help your child classify according to the sense of touch. **GOAL**

MATERIALS

A paper bag to be used as a grab bag, a variety of hard and soft objects — rock, piece of fabric, block, cotton ball, and so on.

PROCEDURE

1. Put the objects in a paper bag.

2. Ask your child to reach into the bag and pull out a hard object.

3. Then ask your child to pull out a soft object.

4. Continue until all the objects are out of the bag.

5. Now ask your child to line up the objects into two groups, one line for hard objects; the other for soft ones.

TIME

Ten to fifteen minutes.

EVALUATION

This activity is a success when your child can distinguish between hard and soft objects.

RELATED ACTIVITY

Put rough and smooth objects in the bag and follow the same procedure.

OBSERVING LEARNING

The best part of this activity for my child was _____

_____

_____

My child's favorite part of this activity was _____

_____

laundry sort □ ◑

GOAL To help your child learn to sort clothing into different groups.

MATERIALS

The family laundry.

PROCEDURE

1. Tell your child that today is a day for fun — sorting the laundry. Suggest that you will sort several ways.

   - you will sort by person (whose clothes they are)
   - you will sort by type of clothing (socks, shirts, pants and so on)
   - you will sort by color
   - you will sort by shape

2. Have your child sort the laundry according to whose clothes they are, and then continue through the various categories.

TIME

About a half hour.

EVALUATION

This activity is a success when your child can successfully sort clothing in two or three different ways.

RELATED ACTIVITY

You can also ask your child to tell you how to sort. If you make a "mistake", can your child catch you?

OBSERVING LEARNING

My child liked this activity because _____

_____

_____

This activity was difficult for my child because _____

_____

_____

9 understanding prepositions

boxes and bags □ ◑

GOAL

To help your child grow in understanding the following prepositions: inside, in front of, over, beside, between.

MATERIALS

Two boxes (large enough for a child to sit in) or two large grocery bags.

PROCEDURE

1. Ask your child to get *inside* the box. Now ask him or her where he or she is. Encourage your child to say, "I am inside the box."

2. Now ask your child to get *in front of* the box. Ask him or her where he or she is. Again encourage him or her to say, "I am in front of the box."

3. Continue in this manner until you and your child have used the words *inside, in front of, over, beside,* and *between.*

TIME

About fifteen minutes.

EVALUATION

This activity is a success when your child can perform the action and then use the correct preposition to describe it.

RELATED ACTIVITY

Do this activity using your child's favorite toy and a shoe box. Put the toy *inside, in front of, over, beside* the box and *between* two boxes.

OBSERVING LEARNING

This activity helped my child because _____

_____

My child's favorite part of this activity was _____

_____

□ ◔

in the bag

To help your child understand and use these prepositions: inside, in front of, over, beside, between.

MATERIALS

Two paper bags and a favorite toy.

PROCEDURE

1. Ask your child to put the toy *inside* the bag and tell you what he or she has done.

2. Now ask your child to put the toy *in front of* the bag. Again have him or her explain the action.

3. Continue in this manner until your child has done the same for each of the words — over, beside, and between.

TIME

About five minutes.

EVALUATION

This activity is a success when your child can put an object where you ask and tell you (using the correct preposition) what he or she has done.

OBSERVING LEARNING

The hardest part of this activity for my child was _____

_____

_____

From doing this activity, my child learned _____

_____

_____

in and out □ ◔

GOAL

To help your child grow in understanding the following prepositions: inside, in front of, over, beside, between.

MATERIALS

A penny and a cup.

PROCEDURE

1. Ask your child to put the penny *inside* the cup and tell you where it is.

2. Now ask your child to put the penny *in front of* the cup. Again have him or her tell you where it is.

3. Next ask your child to put the penny *beside* the cup and tell you where it is.

4. Continue in this manner until all of the prepositions mentioned above have been used.

TIME

About five minutes.

EVALUATION

This activity is a success when your child can put the penny where you ask, and can tell you where it is using the correct prepositions.

RELATED ACTIVITY

Try this activity while preparing dinner. Let your child use a colander and a spoon, or if your child is capable, set the table, telling you where each item goes in relation to the plate.

OBSERVING LEARNING

From doing this activity, my child learned _____

_____

_____

□ ◑ _____ # up and over

To help your child understand words which tell directions. **GOAL**

Your child's favorite toy and an empty shoe box. **MATERIALS**

PROCEDURE

1. Set the box on a table in front of your child.

2. Put the toy *under* the box, telling your child what you did.

3. Now ask your child to repeat what you just did. Encourage your child to tell you what he or she did.

4. Do the same procedure for the following prepositions: over, near, down, up, next to, between, in front of, and in.

TIME

Fifteen to thirty minutes.

EVALUATION

This activity is a success when your child can copy your actions with the toy and tell you what he or she did.

RELATED ACTIVITY

Ask your child to position the toy in relation to the box *without a demonstration from you.* Then have him or her tell you where it is.

OBSERVING LEARNING

The hardest part of this activity for my child was _____

_____

_____

popsicle stick puppet

GOAL   To help your child comprehend the following prepositions: inside, in front of, over, beside, between.

MATERIALS

Popsicle stick or a tongue depressor, glue, person or animal cut out of a coloring book, large truck, one other toy.

PROCEDURE

1. Let your child color the cutout figure, and then help him or her paste it on the popsicle stick.

2. Ask your child to put the stick puppet *inside* the truck, and have him or her tell you where the puppet is.

3. Then ask him or her to put the puppet *in front of* the truck and tell you where it is.

4. Continue in this manner until your child has demonstrated the remaining three prepositions — over, beside, and between. (For the latter, you will need to use the other toy.)

TIME

Fifteen to twenty minutes.

EVALUATION

This activity is a success when your child can use the puppet to demonstrate each preposition.

RELATED ACTIVITY

Let your child use the puppet to give directions to you.

OBSERVING LEARNING

The hardest part of this activity for my child was _____

_____

_____

tubes and tires

GOALS

To help your child experience and comprehend the following prepositions: inside, in front of, beside.

MATERIAL

An old inner tube or tire.

PROCEDURE

1. Demonstrate for your child what it means to stand *inside, in front of,* and *beside* the tube or tire.

2. Now ask your child to stand *inside, in front of,* and *beside* the tube or tire, always asking him or her to tell you where he or she is.

3. Switch roles and allow your child to tell you where to stand in relationship to the tube or tire.

TIME

Fifteen to twenty minutes.

EVALUATION

This activity is a success when your child can "perform" the prepositions using the tube or tire.

OBSERVING LEARNING

My child's favorite part of this activity was _____

_____

_____

I think this activity helped my child because _____

_____

_____

hoops

GOALS To help your child experience and comprehend the following prepositions: inside, in front of, over, beside, between.

MATERIALS

Two plastic hoops about two feet in diameter.

PROCEDURE

1. Lay one hoop down on the floor.

2. Ask your child to jump *inside* the hoop, telling you what he or she is doing.

3. Then have your child use the hoop to demonstrate the prepositions in front of, over, and beside.

4. Now lay two hoops next to each other on the floor, and ask your child to jump *between* them.

5. Switch roles and allow your child to tell you where to jump.

TIME

About fifteen to twenty minutes.

EVALUATION

This activity is a success when your child can "perform" the prepositions with the hoop.

OBSERVING LEARNING

My child's favorite part of this activity was _____

_____

_____

I think this activity helped my child because _____

_____

_____

□ ◑ ──────────────────────────────────── **magnets**

To help your child understand the following prepositions: above, below, beside, between.

GOAL

──────────────────────────────── **MATERIALS**

Magnets (the kind used on the refrigerator or message
board), any metal surface.

──────────────────────────────── **PROCEDURE**

1. Place two magnets on the metal surface and give your
   child one magnet.

2. Ask your child to place his or her magnet *above* your
   magnets.

3. Continue this activity using the prepositions *below*,
   beside and *between*.

4. Change roles. Have your child tell you where to place
   the magnet.

5. Get your child to move the magnet, telling you where he
   or she is placing it in relation to the other magnets.

──────────────────────────────── **TIME**

Ten to fifteen minutes.

──────────────────────────────── **EVALUATION**

This activity is a success when your child is able to correctly place the magnet
for each preposition.

──────────────────────────────── **RELATED ACTIVITY**

Vary the types of magnets using ABC magnets, cartoon figures, or fruits and
vegetables.

──────────────────────────────── **OBSERVING LEARNING**

I think this activity helped my child because ─────────────────

──

water play _____ □ ◑

GOAL To help your child understand the following prepositions: in, out, over, under, beside, between.

MATERIALS _____

A sink or basin, water, and several plastic cups and bowls.

PROCEDURE _____

1. Fill the sink or basin with water.

2. Dip one of the plastic cups in the water and fill it. Then pour the cupful of water into an empty cup.

3. Say to your child as you pour, "I am pouring the water *in* the cup."

4. Ask your child, "Can you pour the water *in* the cup?" and let him or her try.

5. You take a turn and pour and make a mistake. Pour the water *beside* the cup, and ask, "Am I pouring the water *in* the cup?"

6. Ask your child to show you what the cup looks like when the water is *out* of the cup and when the water is *in* the cup.

7. Place your hand *over* the cup and ask your child, "Is my hand *over* the cup?" Do the same for *under*.

8. Repeat this procedure using all the prepositions listed above.

TIME _____

About fifteen minutes.

EVALUATION _____

This activity is a success when your child can understand and use the prepositions.

OBSERVING LEARNING _____

This activity helped my child because _____

_____

_____

chapter 10

remembering what you hear

(auditory memory)

hidden treasure ▢ ◑

GOAL To increase your child's ability to remember what he or she hears.

MATERIALS

Boxes, toys, or articles of clothing.

PROCEDURE

1. Take three to five of these items and hide them around the house or room.

2. Tell your child what you have hidden.

3. Ask your child to find the items by following your directions, but to wait until you finish speaking.

4. Start with a simple two-step direction, follow by giving a three-step direction ([1]Go to the bedroom, [2]look under the bed, and [3]bring me the red ball.); then a four-step direction ([1]Walk into the bathroom, [2]open the door under the sink, [3]look inside the paper bag, and [4]bring me the surprise you find.).

TIME

Ten to fifteen minutes.

EVALUATION

This activity is a success when your child can find an object following first a two-step then a three-step direction.

RELATED ACTIVITY

This activity could be tried with four-year-olds using only one- or two-step directions. Let your child do the hiding and give you the directions.

OBSERVING LEARNING

My child enjoyed this activity because _____

_____

_____

□ ● ———————————————————— # house helpers

GOAL

To increase your child's ability to remember what he or she hears.

MATERIALS

None.

PROCEDURE

1. Ask your child to help fix a meal.

2. Start with simple two-step directions, such as, "Open the refrigerator and bring me the milk." Have your child repeat the directions and then do what was asked.

3. After your child can easily follow two-step directions, move to three-step directions, such as, "Pour the milk in the bowl, stir it up, and add the sugar."

4. After your child can easily follow three-step directions, increase the directions to four steps.

TIME

Thirty to forty minutes.

EVALUATION

This activity is a success when your child can easily follow a four-step direction.

RELATED ACTIVITY

This activity could be easily adapted as a game to encourage your child to pick up his or her toys.

OBSERVING LEARNING

The hardest part of this activity for my child was _____

_____

_____

odds and ends □ ◔

GOAL

To increase your child's ability to remember what he or she hears.

MATERIALS

Common objects found in your home (shoe, place mat, jar, piece of fruit, and so on).

PROCEDURE

1. Put several objects on a table in front of your child.

2. Tell your child to pick up the two objects you name in the order you name them (i.e., "Give me the jar and the place mat.").

3. Make sure your child waits until you finish talking before he or she starts.

4. After your child can remember two objects, ask for three, then four objects.

TIME

About five minutes.

EVALUATION

This activity is a success when your child can remember your directions, giving you, in order, the four objects named.

RELATED ACTIVITY

Let your child select the objects and give you the directions.

OBSERVING LEARNING

The best part of this activity for my child was _____

_____

_____

□ ◑ ——————————————————————— # nursery rhymes

GOAL

To increase your child's ability to remember what he or she hears.

MATERIALS

The poem entitled "The House That Jack Built".

PROCEDURE

1. Read the poem to your child several times.

2. After several readings, encourage your child to begin filling in the familiar parts. Prompt your child when necessary.

TIME

Ten to fifteen minutes.

EVALUATION

This activity is a success when your child can supply three or four parts to the poem.

RELATED ACTIVITIES

There are other poems and songs which contain a sequence that is often repeated, such as "I'm Going on a Lion Hunt" or the "Twelve Days of Christmas". Share them with your child.

OBSERVING LEARNING

My child enjoyed this activity because _____

_____

_____

Another poem we used and liked was _____

_____

_____

alison's raisins

GOAL To increase your child's ability to remember what he or she hears.

MATERIALS

A box of raisins.

PROCEDURE

1. Discuss with your child how your face looks when you feel happy.

2. Using the raisins, make a circle and a "happy face" smile, omitting the nose and two eyes.

3. Tell your child to look at the "happy face" and use a raisin to put a nose where it belongs.

4. Then have your child put raisins where each eye should be.

TIME

Five to ten minutes.

EVALUATION

This activity is a success when your child can listen to your instructions, using the raisins to make a nose and two eyes.

OBSERVING LEARNING

The part of the activity my child liked best was _____
_____
_____

From this activity, my child learned _____
_____
_____

○ ◑ ———————————————————————— # telephone

GOAL

To increase your child's ability to remember what he or she hears.

MATERIALS

None.

PROCEDURE

1. Whisper a silly sentence in your child's ear. (e.g., The cow said "quack" and the duck said "moo".).

2. Now ask your child to repeat it to you.

3. Repeat this game several times, adding and changing parts of the silly sentence.

TIME

Ten to fifteen minutes.

EVALUATION

This activity is a success when your child can repeat the silly sentence exactly as you said it.

RELATED ACTIVITY

This makes a perfect rainy day activity for a small group of children. Alliterative rhymes such as "Peter Piper" may be used for more able children.

OBSERVING LEARNING

The hardest part of this activity for my child was _____

_____

_____

Comments _____

_____

_____

bugging ⬜ ◑

GOAL To increase your child's ability to remember what he or she hears.

MATERIALS

Tape recorder, recording of common everyday sounds (e.g., doorbell, door closing, children talking, vacuum cleaner, washing machine, shower, footsteps, and so on).

PROCEDURE

1. Take a few days to record the sounds onto a tape.
2. Play one sound to your child, telling him or her to listen carefully.
3. Ask your child to identify the sound.
4. Then play two sounds, asking your child to identify each sound.
5. Increase the number of sounds until all sounds are identified.

TIME

Fifteen to twenty minutes.

EVALUATION

This activity is a success when your child is able to correctly recall all sounds played.

RELATED ACTIVITIES

Use the sounds from the playground or a shopping mall or use animal sounds.

OBSERVING LEARNING

A problem my child had with this activity was _____

_____

_____

My child enjoyed this activity because _____

_____

_____

wiggly worm

GOALS

To help your child to listen closely and remember what he or she hears.

MATERIAL

A grassy spot in your backyard or in a nearby park.

PROCEDURE

1. Sit down and pull a blade of grass.

2. Say to your child, "Let's pretend that this blade of grass is a wiggly worm and listen to where he's going."

3. Show and tell your child at the same time a three-step sentence: "Wiggly Worm is going under the leaf, over the rock, and through the grass." or "Wiggly Worm is going under your toe, over your knee, and will tickle your nose."

4. Then ask your child to show and tell you exactly what Wiggly Worm did.

TIME

Ten to twenty minutes.

EVALUATION

This activity is a success when your child can show and retell the three-step sentence.

RELATED ACTIVITIES

A pebble can be used as a bug or a leaf can be used as a butterfly. The places they can go and things they can do are many. After your child can retell three-step activities, increase to four-step and later five-step activities.

OBSERVING LEARNING

My child enjoyed this activity because _____

_____

drummers ☐ ◔

GOAL To help your child remember sounds made in a rhythm he or she hears.

MATERIALS

Drumsticks and a drum or spoons and a pot.

PROCEDURE

1. Using the drum and drumsticks, tap out a simple rhythm (for example: short, short, short, long).

2. Have your child repeat the rhythm.

3. Vary your rhythm and have your child repeat it.

TIME

Five to ten minutes.

EVALUATION

This activity is a success when your child can repeat five different rhythms five times correctly.

RELATED ACTIVITIES

You can use any musical instrument for this activity, or you can try simply clapping your hands or stamping your feet to achieve sounds and rhythm.

OBSERVING LEARNING

This activity helped my child because _____

_____

_____

Comments _____

_____

_____

11

hearing differences in sounds

(auditory discrimination)

kitchen detective □ ◐

GOAL To help your child distinguish various kitchen sounds.

MATERIALS

None.

PROCEDURE

1. At dinnertime, have your child with you in the kitchen as you work.

2. While fixing dinner, say to your child, "Do you want to play a game? Then close your eyes and tell me what sound you hear."

3. While your child's eyes are closed, you could do any one of the following: chop nuts, remove ice cubes from a tray, dial the telephone, boil water in a tea kettle, break eggs, run the electric mixer, and so on.

TIME

Approximately five to fifteen minutes.

EVALUATION

This activity is a success when your child can identify three out of four sounds.

OBSERVING LEARNING

This activity was worthwhile for my child because _____

_____

_____

The part of this activity my child enjoyed the most was _____

_____

_____

clapping words

To help your child listen for syllables of words. **GOAL**

MATERIALS

None.

PROCEDURE

1. Clap the syllables in your child's name, one clap for each syllable. (For example, John is one clap; Sally is two claps.) Say each syllable as you clap.

2. Clap the various family members' names.

3. Now clap the names without saying the name, and ask your child to identify the family member.

TIME

Approximately five to ten minutes.

EVALUATION

This activity is a success when your child can recognize the family names just through the claps (no voice).

RELATED ACTIVITY

Let your child do the clapping and you do the guessing!

OBSERVING LEARNING

The hardest thing about this activity for my child was _____
_____
_____

This activity was helpful to my child because _____
_____
_____

an ABC meal

GOAL   To help your child grow in the ability to hear likenesses and differences in sounds.

MATERIALS

None.

PROCEDURE

1. Next time you are waiting somewhere with your child, pretend you are planning a meal. Name a food that begins with "a".

2. Then have your child name a food that begins with "b".

3. Continue in this manner through the alphabet.

TIME

Fifteen to twenty minutes.

EVALUATION

This activity is a success when your child can give a minimum of five foods for various letters of the alphabet.

OBSERVING LEARNING

The hardest part of this activity for my child was _____

_____

_____

My child enjoyed this activity because _____

_____

_____

"t" train

GOAL

To help your child grow in the ability to hear likenesses and differences in sounds.

MATERIALS

None.

PROCEDURE

1. During a quiet time with your child, play "t" train. Say, "We're going on a train taking only things that begin with the "t" sound. Listen carefully so that we only take things that begin with the "t" sound.

2. Begin to name things that begin with "t", such as top, toy, tomato, and so on. Approximately after every three words mention something that doesn't begin with "t" such as ball.

3. Tell your child to say "stop" everytime you say a word that begins with a different sound.

TIME

Five to ten minutes.

EVALUATION

This activity is a success when your child stops you on the "wrong" sound.

RELATED ACTIVITIES

Any sound your child needs practice in hearing may be used.

OBSERVING LEARNING

The hardest part of this activity for my child was _____

_____

_____

silly sentences

GOAL
To help your child grow in the ability to hear likenesses and differences in sounds.

MATERIALS

None.

PROCEDURE

1. Make up one sentence using as many words containing the "s" sound as possible. For example, say, *Silly Sally saw seven swans.*

2. Now ask your child to make up another sentence using that same sound.

TIME

Five to ten minutes.

EVALUATION

This activity is a success when your child can make up a sentence with a minimum of three words having the same sound.

OBSERVING LEARNING

My child enjoyed this activity because _____

_____

_____

This activity was helpful to my child because _____

_____

_____

□ ◑

where am I?

GOAL

To enable your child to listen carefully and distinguish the direction from which a sound comes.

MATERIALS

Wood blocks, wooden spoons, or pan lids.

PROCEDURE

1. Tell your child you are going to hit two objects together while standing in different areas of the room.

2. Have your child close his or her eyes and tell you from where in the room the noise is coming.

TIME

Fifteen minutes.

EVALUATION

This activity is a success when your child can identify the correct area from which the sound comes.

RELATED ACTIVITY

Have your child sit on a chair with his or her eyes closed. While walking around the chair, move far away and then close to the chair. Have your child tell you how far or near you are by the noise.

OBSERVING LEARNING

This activity was helpful to my child because _____

_____

_____

The hardest part of this activity for my child was _____

_____

_____

city sounds _____ □ ◑

GOAL To help your child tell the difference between loud and soft city noises.

MATERIALS _____

A recording of city noises or a trip with your child to the city.

PROCEDURE _____

1. Tell your child that you are going to play a recording of sounds that are heard in the city.

2. Ask him or her to tell you which noises are loud and which are soft.

TIME _____

Approximately five to fifteen minutes.

EVALUATION _____

This activity is a success when your child can identify which sounds are loud and which are soft.

RELATED ACTIVITIES _____

Use objects to create loud and soft sounds. Also ask your child to identify the sounds and tell you what makes each one.

OBSERVING LEARNING _____

From this activity, my child learned _____

_____

_____

The hardest thing for my child to do in this activity was _____

_____

_____

knock on wood

GOAL

To help your child hear differences in sounds.

MATERIALS

A wooden or metal spoon and objects in the kitchen.

PROCEDURE

1. Have your child cover his or her eyes while you tap with a spoon on various appliances and objects in the kitchen (wood, plastic, metal, glass).

2. Ask your child to identify the object from which the sound is made without looking.

TIME

About ten minutes.

EVALUATION

This activity is a success when your child can correctly identify the objects producing the sounds.

RELATED ACTIVITIES

This activity can be done in other rooms of the house and can be made more complicated by increasing the noise level in the house, i.e., putting on the dishwasher, TV, stereo, or opening windows.

OBSERVING LEARNING

The part of this activity that helped my child the most was _____
_____
_____

My child enjoyed this activity because _____
_____
_____

chapter

12

repeating a story and recalling verbal directions

(auditory retention)

□ ◑ _____ **super soup**

To help your child grow in the ability to remember and repeat what he or she hears.

_____ **MATERIALS**

A can of soup.

_____ **PROCEDURE**

1. Have your child accompany you into the kitchen.

2. Taking the can of soup, read the directions aloud to your child.

3. Now ask your child to repeat the directions, telling you what to do first, second, third and so on in making the soup.

_____ **TIME**

About fifteen minutes.

_____ **EVALUATION**

This activity is a success when your child can repeat to you the steps needed (in order) in preparing a can of soup.

_____ **RELATED ACTIVITIES**

Try this activity when preparing a gelatin dessert or a frozen vegetable.

_____ **OBSERVING LEARNING**

My child enjoyed this activity because _____

_____

_____

From doing this activity, my child learned _____

_____

_____

happy house □ ◑

GOALS

To help your child grow in the ability to remember several directions and follow them.

MATERIALS

Plain paper, crayons.

PROCEDURE

1. Give your child a sheet of paper. Tell him or her to fold it in half.

2. Then have him or her fold it in half again.

3. Have your child open up the paper to reveal four boxes.

4. Handing your child crayons, give specific directions to him or her about what to draw in each box. For example, tell your child to draw a lemon in the first box, a red flower in the second box, a square in the third box, and a brown hat in the fourth box.

TIME

About fifteen minutes.

EVALUATION

This activity is a success when your child can remember the directions and can follow them correctly.

RELATED ACTIVITY

Rather than drawing pictures, your child could cut and paste pictures from magazines onto the four boxes.

OBSERVING LEARNING

The part my child enjoyed the most was _____

_____

_____

□ ◐ ─────────────────────────────────── # tv time

To help your child grow in the ability to remember a story in sequence. **GOAL**

─────────────────────────────── **MATERIALS**

A television set.

─────────────────────────────── **PROCEDURE**

1. Watch your child's favorite TV show with him or her.

2. When the show is over, ask your child the following questions: (a) Who were the characters? (b) What did they do? (c) Why did the show end the way it did?

─────────────────────────────── **TIME**

Forty-five minutes to an hour.

─────────────────────────────── **EVALUATION**

This activity is a success when your child can correctly answer the three questions, given above, concerning the television show.

─────────────────────────────── **RELATED ACTIVITY**

Use a nursery rhyme or a short story and follow the same procedure.

─────────────────────────────── **OBSERVING LEARNING**

The part my child enjoyed the most in this activity was _____

_____

_____

Comments _____

_____

_____

making menus □ ◑

GOALS

To help your child improve his or her memory skills and remember events in sequence.

MATERIALS

Pencils or crayons and several pieces of paper.

PROCEDURE

1. Sit down with your child in the evening and help him or her remember the foods he or she has eaten for each meal that day, beginning with breakfast.

2. As your child names the food, draw on a piece of paper a picture of each food eaten at that meal (cereal, milk, juice, banana).

3. Ask your child sequence questions: Which food was eaten first? second? third? and so on.

4. Ask your child to draw pictures of the foods *in the sequence* they were eaten.

5. Then ask your child which meal did he or she eat next. "What did you eat after breakfast?" "after lunch?" "after snack?" Then repeat steps 2 to 4 for each meal.

TIME

Thirty minutes.

EVALUATION

This activity is a success when your child correctly names the foods in the order eaten for each meal.

RELATED ACTIVITY

Have a collection of pictures of individual foods available. Let your child select the appropriate pictures instead of drawing them.

OBSERVING LEARNING

The hardest part of this activity for my child was _____

_____

_____

□ ◑ _____ # memory mural

To help your child to remember events in order and to reproduce them on a paper.

_____ MATERIALS

Light or white shelf paper about eighteen inches wide and five feet long, crayons.

_____ PROCEDURE

1. After a special event, such as a birthday party, picnic, trip to the zoo, beach or amusement park, spread the shelf paper on the floor and tell your child that he or she is going to draw a mural of the event.

2. Have the child begin at the left and draw each part of the special occasion in the order that each happened. (For example: picking out the present/decorations, dressing for the party, who came, the games, the cake, and going home.)

_____ TIME

About thirty minutes.

_____ EVALUATION

This activity is a success when your child can remember in order three things that happened on a special day, and represent to his or her satisfaction a drawing which symbolizes these things.

_____ OBSERVING LEARNING

From this activity my child learned _____

_____

_____

A problem my child had with this activity was _____

_____

_____

child's version _____ □ ◑

GOAL   To help your child grow in the ability to remember and reproduce what he or she has heard.

MATERIALS _____

A favorite book of your child's, crayons, paper.

PROCEDURE _____

1. Read the book to your child.

2. When you are finished, hand the crayons and paper to your child asking him or her to retell the story by drawing pictures.

3. Encourage your child to remember as much of the story as possible.

TIME _____

About thirty minutes.

EVALUATION _____

This activity is a success when your child can depict the story line through drawings of main characters and events.

RELATED ACTIVITY _____

Let your child try to role play the story after reading the book. He or she can select one character and imitate what the character did in the story.

OBSERVING LEARNING _____

This activity was helpful to my child because _____

_____

_____

My child enjoyed this activity because _____

_____

□ ◑ _____ # taped tales

GOAL

To increase your child's ability to remember what he or she hears.

MATERIALS

A picture book, tape recorder, blank tape.

PROCEDURE

1. Read a picture book to your child. Record your reading on a tape.

2. Then using the book, have him or her tell you the story. Record the child's version on tape.

3. Listen to both versions and discuss any differences between them with your child. If your child's version is accurate, have him or her try to record the story without looking at the picture book.

TIME

A half hour.

EVALUATION

This activity is a success when your child can remember the most important details of the story.

RELATED ACTIVITY

This activity could also be done without a tape recorder. Have your child draw pictures of what he or she remembers, and then retell the story.

OBSERVING LEARNING

My child enjoyed this activity because _____

_____

_____

I think this activity helped my child because _____

_____

grocery help

GOAL To help your child grow in the ability to follow directions.

MATERIALS

None.

PROCEDURE

1. Have your child go with you to the store the next time you plan to shop.

2. Let your child help you put the groceries in your shopping cart. Start by asking your child to put the following three items, in the order you say them, in your cart: a loaf of bread, a package of cheese, and a carton of milk. (All items should be in sight.) Repeat your directions only if necessary.

3. Select four more items you plan to purchase, and ask your child to put them in the cart for you in the order requested.

4. When your child completes the activity, have him or her repeat the items gotten.

TIME

Thirty to sixty minutes.

EVALUATION

This activity is a success when your child can recall what items you asked him or her to find, can put them in your cart in the order you requested, and can then name those items.

RELATED ACTIVITY

This activity can be done on other kinds of shopping trips — going to the toy store or department store.

OBSERVING LEARNING

I think this activity helped my child because _____

_____

_____

□ ◑ ──────────────────────── # plan of attack

GOALS

To help your child grow in the ability to remember and repeat what he or she hears after a period of time has elapsed.

MATERIALS

None.

PROCEDURE

1. In the morning when your child gets up, tell him or her, step-by-step, what you will do that day.

2. Have your child repeat to you the plans for the day.

3. In the evening, review with your child, step-by-step, what activities you did that day.

TIME

Ten to fifteen minutes.

EVALUATION

This activity is a success when your child can repeat all of the day's plans and can recall at the end of the day most of the day's events.

RELATED ACTIVITY

This activity could be simplified to take in only the immediate activity. For example, say to child, "Please get out of bed, brush your teeth, put on your shirt, then your pants, then your socks and shoes, brush your hair, and then come to the kitchen for breakfast."

OBSERVING LEARNING

My child enjoyed this activity because _____

_____

_____

appendix a

CHILDREN WITH SPECIAL LEARNING NEEDS

Learning for most children is as necessary as the intake of food and drink for their life and growth process. However, certain children have problems with learning just as other children have difficulty with eating. Both problems can be caused by a wide variety of conditions and may be indicated by a vast array of different symptoms. A child may have trouble developing healthy eating habits because of improper physical structures, poor nutrition, or allergic reactions. A child may have trouble learning the expected skills in our society because of mental retardation, learning disabilities, or emotional disorders. Each of these types of problems requires diagnosis and intervention by the adults in that child's life if optimal growth and development are to occur.

How Can We Help Children With Special Learning Needs?

The first step in helping the child with learning problems must be the same as the first step in helping the child with physical problems — *securing a specific, indepth diagnosis* by an expert in the field. There are many tests available to physicians, psychologists, and specialists in the mental health field which can help to determine the exact nature of a child's learning problem. Just as a child with a stomach ulcer is not likely to grow well if he or she is treated with guesswork, so too will the child who suffers from a perceptual-motor learning disability not be able to do well if no specific help is provided.

Once the learning disability is diagnosed, a particular treatment may be prescribed or recommended. Very often, the activities presented in this book will provide complementary activities to a specialized treatment program. As such, they may be called "prescriptive teaching" because, like prescriptive medicine, they provide a remedy based on a specific, professional diagnosis of the problem. They are easy activities which can help a child strengthen or build a learning skill in an enjoyable interaction with parent or teacher.

How Can This Book Help Special Needs Learners?

What this book does is look at the kinds of skills necessary for school success and beginning literacy, break them down into small parts, and prescribe activities based on the way children normally learn these skills in the course of their development. Young children from ages two to four will often show a natural, intense interest in many of these skills. Many of them are just learning the meaning of prepositions and how to categorize. They can be heard to say "up" and "down" as they manipulate toys in their play, and you will see them group toys according to "mine" and "yours".

Older children with special needs may have a very hard time with these same skills. In choosing activities for your special needs child, look closely at his or her learning patterns and then introduce an activity designed to strengthen a particular skill. If, for example, he or she has a hard time with listening skills, select activities which will help with remembering, repeating, and discriminating sounds and stories.

If your child moves quickly through an activity with interest, try a related activity. If your child resists, offer a similar alternative or one that he or she choses. Present any activity as something that's fun for you both and that you both enjoy doing.

If the activity seems too difficult for your child and you see that he or she is becoming frustrated, then adjust it to your child's abilities. Breaking a task into a series of smaller tasks to be mastered one at a time usually will work. Sometimes if the adult models or specifically shows the child how to do a task, then the child can more easily copy the behavior. Don't force a child who is frustrated or refuses to participate to go through the steps just for the sake of completion. Try the activity some other time, try an alternative activity, try modeling, and try encouragement — lots of encouragement!

The activities in *I'm Ready to Learn* provide a variety of simple steps designed to reinforce the basic skills needed for school success. They are simple enough that they require no special training by parent or volunteer, yet they provide an interesting use of everyday materials. The games and activities can be a starting point for teachers and parents who wish to create their own activities, making adjustments for their unique environment and their unique children.

Using These Activities With the Educationally Mentally Retarded

Usually, children who are educationally mentally retarded need more repetition of a learning task than average learners, and they require breaking down a particular task into smaller, simpler steps.[1] Present the first step. Once it has been mastered, present the second step — a few hours later or on another day. Wait for your child to experience success with each step before moving on to the next one. Look at each step as an accomplishment — a treasure. Challenges must be balanced with patience; struggles with encouragement.

Although all of the chapters could be helpful to the child who is educationally mentally retarded or a slow learner, the following general preacademic skills would be especially valuable: Remembering Order and Placement of Shapes (Chapter 2), Labeling (Chapter 7), Grouping and Describing (Chapter 8), and Understanding Prepositions (Chapter 9).

appendix a

Using These Activities With Children Who Have Learning Disabilities

Learning disabled children are usually considered to have difficulty with some types of skills but not with others.[2] The child who suffers from a visual perception problem would benefit from activities which specifically work on the building of visual skills such as those presented in Chapter 1: Remembering What You See, Chapter 2: Remembering Order and Placement of Shapes, Chapter 3: Seeing the Same Shape When It Has Been Moved, Chapter 4: Reproducing Simple Designs and Patterns, and Chapter 6: Seeing and Describing Large and Small Details.

A child who has a visual motor learning disability would most likely benefit from activities in Chapter 5: Large and Small Muscle Control and Chapter 4: Reproducing Simple Designs and Patterns.

The child with auditory learning problems will gain the most from activities in Chapter 10: Remembering What You Hear, Chapter 11: Hearing Differences in Sounds, and Chapter 12: Repeating a Story and Recalling Verbal Directions.

In summary, then, the activities in this book represent a breakdown or task analysis of skills required for school success into smaller, more manageable tasks. School success usually depends on the development of skills which are hierarchial and cumulative in nature. In this book, prereadiness activities such as "Reproducing Simple Designs and Patterns" provide the foundation and building blocks for later school activities such as writing ABCs or C-A-T. Development of these readiness for learning skills *at an early age* is highly recommended for researchers and theoreticians, especially for children with learning problems, so that later successful school adjustment can be possible.

[1]Blake, K.A. *Educating Exceptional Pupils.* Addison-Wesley Publishing Company, Menlo Park, CA, 1981.

[2]Hallahan, D.P. and T. M. Kauffman. *Introduction to Learning Disabilities — A Psycho-Behavioral Approach.* Prentice Hall, Inc., Englewood Cliffs, N.J., 1976.

OBSERVING LEARNING

ACTIVITY _____

Child's Name	Date	Check for Success	Strengths or Special Comments	Problems or Difficulties

bibliography

Books for Parents and Teachers

Beck, Joan. *How To Raise a Brighter Child.* Pocket Books, New York, 1975.
This book is full of practical, realistic activities with specific descriptions for parents to do in order to stimulate their child's intellect.

Beram, Sandy. *Games On the Go.* Collier Books, New York, 1979.
No family should go on a car trip without this book. Over 150 activities are listed to help take the boredom off travel for children.

Boston Children's Medical Center and E. Gregg. *What to Do When There's Nothing to Do.* Dell Publishing, New York, 1968.
This book provides a wealth of simple activities for parents/caregivers to try with children. It's one of the few books with activities and suggestions for infants.

Brosnaham, JoAnne, and Barbara Milne. *A Calendar of Home/School Activities.* Scott, Foresman and Company, Glenview, IL, 1978.
This book is designed to be used by teachers and parents of children in grades K-3. Each month of the year has a list of activities for parents to do at home. There are a number of creative writing suggestions.

Gambrell, Linda, and Robert Wilson. *28 Ways to Help Your Child Be a Better Reader.* Instructo/McGraw-Hill, Malvern, PA, 1977.
The authors present a myriad of ideas and techniques for parents to help their child in reading. Ideas and concepts covered include reading, advertising, and traffic signs.

Granowsky, Alvin. *A Guide for Better Reading.* Tarmac, Inc., Asheville, NC, 1977.
Dr. Granowsky breaks down the skill of reading into very manageable subskills for parents. In a clear, concise manner, he lists at least three ways parents can reinforce any reading skill.

Harleson, Randy. *Amazing Days.* Workman Publishing, New York, NY, 1979.
This is an activity book for nine- to thirteen-year-olds. Each day of the year has a suggested activity to try.

Lorton, Mary Baratta. *Workjobs For Parents.* Addison-Wesley, Menlo Park, CA, 1975.
This is an excellent book for parents of four- to seven-year-olds. A wide variety of manipulative activities for children are pictured and described.

Ryan, Bernard. *How to Help Your Child Start School.* Perigee Books (C. P. Putnam's & Son), New York, NY, 1980.
This book is an asset for parents of preschoolers, offering specific ways to help four- and five-year-olds get ready for a major turning point in their lives.

White, Burton L. *A Parent's Guide to the First Three Years.* Prentice Hall, Inc., Englewood Cliffs, NJ, 1980.
This will certainly be a book useful to parents of very young children. It's well worth reading — particularly the chapter on play.

Wolfgang, Charles, Bea Mackinder, and Mary E. Wolfgang. *Growing & Learning Through Play.* Instructo/McGraw-Hill, Malvern, PA, 1981.
This book provides a wide variety of play and art activities for parents and teachers of preschool children. The activities presented include structured to open-ended types of play based on children's varied interests and on their patterns of development.

Mother Goose and Nursery Rhymes

Bodecker, N.M. *It's Raining, Said John Twaining.* Atheneum Publishers, New York, NY, 1973.

Briggs, Raymond. *The Mother Goose Treasury.* Coward-McCann and Geoghegan, Inc., New York, NY, 1966.

De Angeli, Marguerite. *The Book of Nursery and Mother Goose Rhymes.* Doubleday & Co., Inc., New York, NY, 1954.

Fujikawa, Gyo. *Mother Goose.* Platt & Munk, New York, NY, 1968.

Greenaway, Kate. *Mother Goose, or The Old Nursery Rhymes.* Frederick Warne & Co., Inc., New York, NY, n.d.

Grover, Eulalie Osgood. *Mother Goose, The Classic Volland Edition.* Rand McNally & Co., Chicago, IL, 1981.

Rojankovsky, Feodor. *The Tall Book of Mother Goose.* Harper & Row, New York, NY, 1942.

Scarry, Richard. *Best Mother Goose Ever.* Golden Press, New York, NY, 1970.

Tarrant, Margaret. *Nursery Rhymes.* Thomas Y. Crowell, New York, NY, 1978.

Tudor, Tasha. *Mother Goose.* Henry Z. Walck, Inc., New York, NY, 1944.

Wright, Blanche Fisher. *The Real Mother Goose.* Rand McNally & Co., Chicago, IL, 1965.